BEYOND THE BRASS PLATE

By the same author:
Gumboot Practice
Dales Law

Beyond the Brass Plate

Stories from a Dales Solicitor

John Francis

Illustrated by Ron Tiner

Smith Settle

First published in 1993 by
Smith Settle Ltd
Ilkley Road
Otley
West Yorkshire
LS21 3JP

ISBN Paperback   1 85825 014 5
1 85825 015 3

British Library Cataloguing-in-Publication Data:
A catalogue record for this book is available
from the British Library.

Designed, printed and bound by
SMITH SETTLE
Ilkley Road   Otley   West Yorkshire LS21 3JP

This book is dedicated to my three children, now young adults, in recognition of their remarkable patience, tolerance and good humour in listening to my oft-repeated jokes, stories and reminiscences over the years.

Acknowledgements

I gratefully acknowledge the help and advice I have received from many people in the course of writing this book, not least from my own family, and my partners, staff and clients. I am particularly indebted to my secretary Sue for all her hard work and skill in deciphering and typing my manuscript.

I have quoted various lawyers, poets, writers, naturalists and sportsmen, who may be beyond the reach of copyright but are certainly not beyond the courtesy of an acknowledgement. I am most grateful to them all.

Author's Note

In these stories there are references to real Yorkshire places, but the reader will not find Denley on any map, for it is an amalgam of the different towns and villages in which I have practised over the years. The people described are composites or wholly imaginary too, but will be familiar to many practising solicitors as 'character types'. I am not in the business of writing unauthorised biographies.

Contents

Friends and Neighbours

The Lord above may have made man to help his neighbour, but in practice man very often does not. From a solicitor's point of view this is rather a comforting fact, for the steady flow of work which comes from neighbour disputes helps to keep him busy.

As a boy in the 1950s I well remember singing along with Max Bygraves that 'with friends and neighbours you're the richest man in town'. Lawyers, however, tend to see the people who do not get on with theirs. There are of course many who are kind to their neighbours, but I strongly suspect that only a minority positively like the folk next door, a larger number just tolerate them and an equally large number either do not communicate at all, live in a state of what might be termed 'armed neutrality' or, in the cases we lawyers see, are in a continuous state of war.

The commonest causes of disputes between neighbours are - in no particular order of popularity - children, animals, boundary walls and fences, shared drives, musical tastes, noise, DIY projects, parking, rubbish, building designs and practices, extensions, gutters, overhanging trees, obsessive curiosity in each other's business, and even on occasion an excessive interest in each other's spouses. This is by no means a comprehensive list, and, for a select few, the absence of a genuine cause of complaint against their neighbour will be no deterrent: they will simply invent one!

On the very day just over thirty years ago when I started my career in law as a very raw articled clerk with Boothroyd and Lytton in the Dales market town of Denley, I was to learn immediately and in dramatic fashion that neighbour disputes were a regular feature of the practice. I have told before in my first book *Gumboot Practice* that my principal, Phillip Lytton, a wise and experienced if somewhat unorthodox Yorkshire solicitor, did not stand on ceremony when it came to putting articled clerks to work. He strongly believed that the best way for them to learn fast was to throw them in at the deep end.

After a brief introduction to the staff, Phillip took me into his office. His idea was that I should learn how to handle clients by watching how he did it, but after a short time he said:

'I'm just popping out for a few minutes to see the bank manager - you're in charge, John.'

Hardly had he left the building when Jayne, the office receptionist, buzzed through on the intercom.

'There's a Mr Stan Fearnley on the line wanting to speak to Mr Lytton urgently. He was very angry when I told him he'd just gone out and he's insisting on speaking to someone else. Mr Lytton said I was to put through any calls to you, so will you speak to him please?'

'Well, I ... er', I began in reply, but before I could collect my thoughts I discovered a very angry farmer at the other end of the line.

'Na then - Mr Francis, i'n't it? - Ah wanted tae speak tae Mr Lytton, like, but t' lass says 'e's not theer - a bloody likely tale, them's me sentiments anyroad! Ah've gitten missen a reight job 'ere - Ah 'opes tha can bloody well 'elp us.'

'I'll do what I can, Mr Fearnley', I replied with as much confidence as I could muster. 'What exactly is your problem?'

'Me neighbour Charley Ford, 'e's me bloody problem', replied Stan, "is sheep are trespassin' on me land agin - they're all ovver t' bloody place. For t' last fifteen year it's bin goin' on - Mr Lytton kens all about t' job, like. An' now Ah've 'ad enuf on it - sae cum on Mr Francis, tell us best way tae sooart t' bugger out?'

As I listened to Stan's tirade I rapidly realised that I was almost certainly on a hiding to nothing in attempting to advise on what was obviously a long-running and intractable problem. I became increasingly nervous and apprehensive.

By a stroke of good luck, however, I had just happened to be reading a law students' notebook on the subject of animal trespass a couple of nights before. One particular remedy stuck in my mind. So without considering either the form or effect of my reply, I blurted out:

'Distress damage feasant - that's your answer Mr Fearnley.'

There was a short silence at the other end of the line before Stan reacted to what was clearly to him a deeply unfamiliar phrase.

'What the bloody 'ell's that when it's at 'ome - tha'd best not be playin' silly buggers wi' me, lad!'

Stan was clearly getting angrier by the minute, so I quickly replied.

'Well, what it means, Mr Fearnley, is that you should round up Mr Ford's sheep which are trespassing on your land, keep them locked up in one of your farm buildings, make sure they're fed and watered properly and don't release them until Mr Ford has settled up with you for the cost of the feed and for any damage they've caused. If he doesn't learn to keep his sheep on his own land in future, then you must speak to Mr Lytton or me and as a last resort we can apply for an injunction.'

'Reight, lad', replied Stan. 'Ah'm off tae put them sheep i' one o' me out'ouses like tha says, Mr Francis, an t' way Ah'm feelin' about t' job, Ah'll 'appen fasten Charley in wi 'em an' all.'

He put the phone down before I could warn him that this last course of action was definitely not part of my advice.

A few weeks later Phillip Lytton had been seeing Stan on some other business and he smiled as he said to me:

'I gather you gave Stan Fearnley a little law lecture on the subject of distress damage feasant. He was quite impressed - once he knew what you were on about!'

I winced slightly at these last words, but I knew that I had already learnt my first lesson in the practice of law - as opposed to the theory of it - when it comes to dealing with Yorkshire farmers: they are not interested in technical expositions of the law, they look for straightforward advice and the more bluntly this is expressed the better.

The day after I had told Stan Fearnley all about distress damage feasant, I found myself once again advising on a neighbour dispute.

Phillip Lytton had gone out of the office to see a farmer up the dale and once again he had left instructions with Jayne to put through any telephone calls to me.

Freddy Jackman was a retired railway worker whose pride and joy was his small vegetable garden at the back of his cottage. Living next door to him was a spinster called Mavis Cockburn who was noted for her obsessive love for all the cats in the locality, especially the seven she owned herself. Freddy did not appreciate the fact that Mavis' cats used his beloved vegetable patch as a public convenience - as he immediately made clear to me when I took his call.

'Them cats 'ave bin at it agin', he began.

'Been at what, Mr Jackman?', I asked.

'Why, usin' me garden as a bog 'ole, that's what, lad! Theer Ah were thinnin' out me carrots, like, when Ah puts me 'and in sum soil at t' side o' t' row, an' t' next minute it's plastered wi' you know what. Fair plastered it were, Mr Francis. Ah reckon it's bin goin' on for long enuf 'as this job. Ah could murder them cats. Is there owt tha can do for us, like? That ginger tom's t' worst o' t' lot if tha wants my opinion.'

I smiled to myself before replying, because Freddy's last words reminded me of a catchphrase from *Ray's a Laugh*, one of my favourite radio comedy programmes when I was a boy: 'It's that ginger tom from next door!' I decided, however, to reply to Freddy with a straight bat. Trying humour on clients can be risky, for they cannot be relied upon to see the funny side of things.

'I'm afraid there is no legal obligation to keep cats under control, as there is for dogs, because cats are considered to have a natural instinct to wander.'

'That dun't seem reight tae me like, Mr Francis', replied Freddy. 'Anyroad, summat 'll 'ave to be dun. Ah reckon Ah'll 'ave tae tackle t' job missen.'

4

Before I could advise Freddy about the dangers of taking the law into his own hands, he put the telephone down.

Although I have always been a dog lover rather than a cat person I was quite worried about the fate of Mavis' cats - particularly her ginger tom - for some time afterwards.

The cases of Stan Fearnley and Freddy Jackman were for me an early introduction to neighbour disputes, and were classics of their kind. It is one thing to act for people like Stan and Freddy, it is quite another matter when the two warring neighbours are both clients and friends! In these situations I am always uneasy, for I know very well that when friends of mine who live next door to each other fall out, I will not feel able to act for either of them. I like to keep my friends.

So far I have managed to retain my two good friends David Endersby and Mike Sewell as clients, even though they live next door to each other and have done for many years.

Both men commute to Bradford every day from their adjoining semi-detached houses in a leafy part of Denley. They share the same office at the wool textile firm where they have both worked as senior executives for many years. Their wives are also firm friends, and one way and another the two couples spend a lot of time in each other's company, being members of the same tennis club, the same amateur dramatic society and having spent many holidays together.

Now for as long as I can remember, David and Mike have enjoyed playing practical jokes on one another. It all started some years ago with an exchange of what were apparently 'official' letters. David sent one to Mike which purported to come from his local council to the effect that half of his garden was being compulsorily purchased to provide a municipal dog loo.

Mike saw through that one, and responded by arranging with a pal of his at the council to send David a similarly official-looking letter informing him that an archaeological dig was shortly to commence in his garden.

There was no stopping David and Mike after that. The majority of the ensuing jokes they played on one another seemed to centre on their gardens, for both men were keen gardeners. Indeed every year

I have the invidious job of inspecting their gardens and pronouncing one a winner. Any solicitor who wishes to keep all his clients should avoid judging competitions like the plague!

Now David has always had a particular hatred of garden gnomes, and on the morning of the day fixed for one of my annual inspections, he looked out of his bedroom window only to be met with the appalling sight of twenty gnomes - of varied size and appearances - fishing in his ornamental pond, all put there by Mike at dead of night. The next year when I was again to judge the gardens, David got his revenge by planting scores of extremely garish artificial flowers in Mike's prize asparagus bed.

If David and Mike were able to laugh at each other's garden jokes, they were not able to laugh quite so quickly or easily when their humour strayed beyond this recognised territory. I was made embarrassingly aware of this fact when I called one day to see David at his office in order to obtain his signature to an urgent legal document. When I went into the office I found David and Mike together. There was an atmosphere of high tension and the expression on David's face was one of absolute fury. It transpired that David had arrived at his office that day to find a letter marked 'Personal and Strictly Private' on his desk. He opened it and read on his company's notepaper a letter purporting to come from the managing director. Now David and Mike had complained to me many times over the years about their employers' meanness when it came to pay rises, but when David read the letter he couldn't believe just how tight-fisted they were.

'We have to inform you that in the particular financial circumstances which prevail and the adverse market conditions now being experienced, it is difficult for the Company to give any salary increase this year, but taking account of all your hard work and commitment and in order to provide you with some strong encouragement and incentive we have decided to award you a rise of 0.01%.'

As he finished reading the letter, David snorted with disbelief. It was at this moment I was shown into his office.

'Just look at this John!', he shouted at me. 'Just look! I've told you about this outfit and its meanness before, but this just about takes the bloody biscuit!'

I read the letter and said rather lamely:'It's not very much, is it?'

'Not very much!?', shouted David again. 'It's a bloody disgrace! I'm going straight in to see the boss right now.'

David started to make his way to the managing director's office when Mike, who had been very quiet whilst his friend ranted and raved, spoke for the first time.

'I wouldn't go in there if I were you', he said.

'Well - have you seen this?', asked David, waving the letter in his friend's face.

'I should have, 'cos I wrote it', replied Mike, rocking with laughter.

For one awful moment I thought I might have to physically separate the two as David moved menacingly towards his friend. His expression went through the full gamut of human emotions before he finally came to terms with his friend's joke.

'Well, you rotten bastard', he eventually exclaimed. 'You know just how to wind me up, don't you?'

I decided the time was now right for me to intervene.

'Now come on you two, remember the old Max Bygraves song - "When you've got friends and neighbours, you're the richest man in town".'

I am still waiting to hear of David's revenge for Mike's great pay rise joke, but revenge there will certainly be. Perhaps I will hear of it the next time I judge their gardens.

Perfect Strangers

I couldn't help but smile to myself when I heard that Reg Ferndale and Margaret Wood were to live next door to each other in the small Dales village of Landersby, for two more different people it would be hard to imagine.

I had known them both practically all my life, Reg through a shared love of fishing and the countryside, Margaret through the local church and amateur dramatic society.

If you define a countryman as one who accepts that nature is 'red in tooth and claw', who knows how to shoot a rabbit or catch a trout, who can grow his own vegetables, who is no stranger to walling, scything or mole-catching, and whose whole being is in tune with the rhythms of the seasons and the weather, then Reg was unquestionably a countryman, for at the age of fifty he could do all these things and more.

It is said in the dale that when Reg was a young man he had quite a reputation with the ladies. There had been someone special, but when she started seeing someone else, he had vowed to have 'nowt tae do wi' t' lasses'. So far as the dalesfolk were concerned he had become a confirmed bachelor, and remained one.

Reg was one of the last breed of a certain type of Englishman - independent, practical and able to turn his hand to anything. He made his living by doing jobbing work for farmers. His services were always greatly in demand, for there was hardly a job of any kind to do with land or stock which he could not do, and do extremely well.

He could be breaking a horse one day, building up a gap in a drystone wall the next day and laying drains the day after. Although years of hard physical work had taken their toll, he was still a fine figure of a man - tall, strong and handsome in a rugged sort of a way. Whenever I saw him he was always dressed in britches, overcoat, muffler and cloth cap, which partially concealed his brown, weather-beaten face.

Margaret, like Reg, had never married, for she had devoted her life to looking after her invalid mother Winifred. Now Winifred was well-known as something of a hypochondriac and she was extremely possessive of her daughter. She was obsessed by her pills, her medical treatment and her diet. She demanded constant attention from her daughter, with the inevitable result that Margaret's social life was extremly limited to say the least. It was perhaps only her involvement with the amateur dramatic society, and with the church where she had been a Sunday school teacher for many years, which kept her from losing her sanity.

After her mother's death, it took Margaret a little time to adjust to the freedom which she had been denied for so long. After giving it a great deal of thought, she decided that she could not make a break from her past by continuing to live in her mother's home, and so she decided - wisely, in my opinion - to sell it and buy her own cottage. She instructed me to act for her in the conveyancing. I was intrigued, and I must say a little concerned, when I discovered that the cottage she had chosen was in Landersby and right next door to my old friend Reg.

At all events, Margaret had made her decision, the purchase of her cottage was completed, and she took up a full-time teaching post at a nearby school where she had taught on a part-time basis for many years.

For a woman in her mid-forties, Margaret was remarkably well-preserved, for she still possessed a trim figure, a relatively unlined face and a good head of curly black hair which had only recently become slightly flecked with silver. Only a year previously she had pleasantly surprised the audience - particularly the male part - by revealing a decent pair of legs when she appeared in the chorus at a pantomime staged by her dramatic society. All in all she remained quite an attractive woman.

Reg and Margaret were both in their very different ways extremely strong characters. I knew very well that there were likely to be problems between the blunt-speaking countryman and the equally forthright schoolmistress who were perfect strangers to each other in every sense. Their first quarrel as neighbours was not long in coming, and it was about rabbits.

Reg, who had the countryman's natural instinct for and love of shooting, was in the habit of 'potting' rabbits in the field adjoining his cottage. Margaret, who for years had taught the children at her Sunday school class that it was wrong to kill any of God's creatures, decided to tackle her neighbour one evening just before dusk, as he made his way home carrying his gun and with a brace of freshly-shot rabbits slung over his shoulder.

'Mr Ferndale, have you got permission to shoot these lovely furry creatures? How can you bear to kill them? Don't you feel guilty?'

Reg did not take at all kindly to being spoken to in this manner by his new neighbour, but he put it down to ignorance and prejudice, that deadly combination which tends to dominate the thinking of those who criticise country ways. Margaret, he reckoned, was ignorant in more ways than one: Joe Stean, the farmer who owned the field, was not only a close friend of Reg, but had been grateful to him for years for his practical help in keeping the rabbit population down. Reg knew that if his new neighbour complained, Joe would give her very short shrift indeed, so he paused for a minute, rested his gun and the dead rabbits on the ground, slowly lit his pipe and then turned to face Margaret.: ''appen tha'd best speak wi t' farmer, Mr Stean, if Ah'm botherin' thee, Miss Wood.'

Margaret turned on her heel and went straight back inside her cottage. What a cruel, uncaring, ignorant man, she thought to herself.

A week later, Margaret saw Reg coming back from the river with four decent-sized trout in his basket.

'Killing things again I see, Mr Ferndale', Margaret couldn't resist calling out to him as he made his way homewards.

Reg did not show his extreme irritation, but grinned cheerfully before replying with just four words:

'This is me supper.'

A few minutes later, Margaret couldn't help but feel slightly envious of her neighbour as the smell of freshly cooked fish came wafting over her as she stood in her garden.

Then there was politics. Reg was conservative in all things, and was inclined to the view commonly held among country people that change in any form was bound to be for the worst; whereas Margaret believed with all the passion of her Christian soul that every person, no matter how evil, was capable of redemption and that the only fair and acceptable society was a socialist one. Margaret was a lady who held very strong political convictions, most of which she had learnt from her mother.

In short, Reg believed in God, Queen and Country; Margaret's creed was republican, pacifist and socialist. It was not very long before they were arguing politics over the dividing hedge as they worked in their respective gardens.

'How can a working man like you possibly support the Tories?', Margaret asked him one day as he was hoeing among his vegetables. 'What have they ever done for you? All they're interested in is money and privilege.'

Reg disregarded the rather patronising nature of his neighbour's question before replying with one of his own.

'Ah'd be reight interested, Miss Wood, if tha can tell us wheer socialism 'as worked anywheer in t' world.'

And so the arguments flew back and forth across the boundary hedge. Reg was for private enterprise, Margaret for state ownership; Reg was for capital punishment, Margaret, predictably, was against it; Reg was for England and all things English, Margaret was for a new world order where nationalism would disappear.

The gardens the two neighbours worked in, as they argued about politics and put the world to rights in their contrasting ways, could not have been more different either.

Reg's was laid out with military precision. His bedding-out plants and vegetables were set in neat geometrical rows and there was not a weed in sight.

Margaret's, on the other hand, was a real cottage garden, full of aromatic pinks and herbs, and herbacious plants, with old-fashioned climbing roses and honeysuckle round the door. Her conservatory, where she spent a lot of her spare time and which was her pride and joy, was a riot of leaf and colour, full of geraniums and various exotic house plants.

Reg and Margaret continued to argue about politics over their boundary hedge. But soon they began to admire each other's gardening skills - and this secret mutual admiration did not end there.

Margaret, who had never previously had the time, opportunity or inclination to become seriously interested in men, suddenly found herself - albeit rather unwillingly - strangely attracted to the blunt-speaking Dalesman who was her neighbour. He was everything she was not, and his values and beliefs were diametrically opposed to everything she had always held dear, yet she could not help herself admiring his rugged physique, his practical know-how and his ability to cook and generally look after himself.

Reg, for his part, had to admit to himself that he was attracted by Margaret's lovely speaking voice - even though he disagreed with most of what she said - her class, her physical appearance and her obvious care and concern - if naïvely expressed - for humanity, for nature and for the countryside.

Two events were to occur which brought Reg's and Margaret's feelings into sharper focus.

Early one morning, as Reg was enjoying his first cup of tea of the day, he was disturbed in his kitchen by the sound of a woman shouting at the top of her voice. He rushed out of the house, and found Magaret standing outside her front door screaming loudly and with an expression of absolute horror on her face. She was watching two magpies attacking a thrush - which Reg knew was Margaret's favourite songbird.

'Do something! Don't just stand there looking, Mr Ferndale, please do something now or the brutes will kill it!'

Reg immediately dashed back into his cottage to get his gun, and seconds later the two magpies had been shot dead.

Margaret's face betrayed the mixture of emotions she felt as she looked at the dead birds, but eventually she blurted out:

'I'm glad you did that, Mr Ferndale.'

Reg, who had been aware all his life of the enormous damage done by magpies to the songbird population, just nodded as he went back to his cottage to finish his early morning cup of tea.

Not long after the magpie shooting, Reg was fly-fishing on the local river one evening when he was suddenly interrupted by the unmistakeable sound of his neighbour's voice.

'Can I have a go, Mr Ferndale?'

'It's all yours, Miss Wood', replied Reg as he handed her his rod.

He thought to himself that he must be mad to let Margaret loose with his venerable and highly-prized Hardy rod.

Predictably, Margaret's first three casts landed in the trees. After Reg had carefully disentangled the line on each occasion, he led Margaret into a nearby field where he gave her a demonstration and a few tips which came from a lifetime of fly fishing, and then made her practise casting for half an hour.

Eventually he said, 'Na then, Miss Wood, let's see if tha can catch us summat for tea.'

After a little while by the river bank Reg lit his pipe, for he could see that Margaret had become engrossed. Not only that, but he could also see that his neighbour was what he'd call a 'natural' in the way that she was combining hand, rod and eye.

'She's really fishing now', he thought to himself.

It was not long before Margaret caught her first trout. It was just undersize and had to be put back. Margaret noted to herself the care with which Reg, like any good fisherman, unhooked the fish and held it gently in the water facing upstream until it was ready to swim away.

'Na then, Miss Wood, that'll do for a start. Ah'm hungry.'

Together they took the brace of half pound trout which Reg had caught earlier back to his cottage. Margaret relaxed in a chair whilst Reg gutted them, cooked them and finally served them in style on his best dinner plates.

This was the first time either had been in the other's home, and although they ate, drank and talked well into the evening, there was still an air of awkwardness between them. They still called each other Mr Ferndale and Miss Wood.

After the evening of 'Margaret's fishing lesson' they started to see more of each other, going fishing together and finding the need more and more frequently to consult each other on various gardening problems.

It was in the garden that the ice between them was finally broken. They were both out working one day, Reg among his vegetables and Margaret among her herbs. Both were suffering from heavy colds.

After they had listened to each other sniffing, sneezing and coughing for quite some time, Margaret suddenly and without thinking called out over the boundary fence:

'Mr Ferndale, I really think we should both be in bed.'

She immediately realised what she had just said and blushed. As she did so, Reg burst out laughing, and the look of acute embarrassment on Margaret's face turned very quickly to a rather naughty smile.

After that the romance blossomed, and soon the new couple's courtship became the talk of the dale. It seemed to have given them a new lease of life, as they began to share each other's very different interests. In no time Margaret became an expert flyfisher - as Reg had predicted - and they went for long walks together when Reg would tutor Margaret in the ways of the country and changing pattern of the seasons. Margaret, for her part, exposed Reg to the joys of art and music. They made an unlikely couple as Margaret led this rugged Dalesman round the local art galleries, patiently explaining each picture and sculpture to him. They also enjoyed their long winter evenings by Margaret's fire as she played selections from her classical music recordings. Reg soon became a passionate admirer of the work of Elgar and Britten.

Twelve months to the day from when they met, Reg asked Margaret to marry him. She accepted, and I was delighted to be invited to the wedding and even more honoured to propose the toast to 'the bride and groom'.

The Settle Record

Occasionally a solicitor in a general country practice finds himself involved in matters far removed from ordinary conveyancing, probate, litigation, neighbour disputes and clients marrying one another.

The strange but intriguing story I am about to tell links one of my favourite Yorkshire towns, the rather special and beautiful chalk-hill blue butterfly, and one of my best-loved character clients.

I have always had a particular affection for Settle, with its narrow streets and alleys, its quaint buildings and grey-stone cottages set in the midst of limestone fells, ever since the day when as a small boy I climbed to the top of Castleberg and sat by the tall flagpole. My eyes followed the top of the cliff to the green hills around the town, dotted with sheep and marked by limestone scars, all the way down to the busy town itself dominated by the Shambles, the Folly and the market place where an old cross stood. In my mind's eye I still see the limestone scars behind Castleberg, containing caves where men and wild animals lived at the dawn of time, and where Roman coins and the bones of reindeer, brown bears and lynx have been found.

I remember Settle, too, for the friendly Yorkshire audience at the Victoria Hall, where for several years as a student I took part in the town's annual drama festival. One year I glowed inwardly when the adjudicator described me as a 'promising young actor'. His one criticism was that I had not portrayed the homosexual side of the character I was playing with much authenticity. I was somewhat relieved by this comment, particularly as a girlfriend was sitting in the front row!

The town and its surrounding countryside are full of magic and mystery. A stone's throw from Settle is Giggleswick School, where I once opened the batting for Rossall Colts on the delightful cricket ground surrounded by a number of lovely old buildings dominated by the green-domed chapel.

Near Giggleswick I once stopped to look at the mysterious Ebbing and Flowing Well. I was lucky enough to see the well in action - I know many have not done so after several visits. I watched in awe as the water in the trough, shielded by sycamores, was one minute filled with leaves and rubbish, the next minute it was all gone only to refill ten minutes later. Sometimes the process takes an hour, other times only minutes. Nobody to my knowledge has ever fully understood or explained it since the phenomenon was first recorded in 1612, but it is thought to be caused by a natural double syphon somewhere in the limestone.

I have over the years spent a lot of my time walking in that marvellous, limestone country which lies between Settle, Malham and upper Wharfedale. It has always appeared to me to be a landscape which has been there since time began, a lost world where one can imagine any number of rare plants, animals and insects being present.

The whole area is rich in its flora and fauna, and there are some very scarce flowers and butterflies: the lady's slipper orchid at Grassington, the brown argus at Buckden, the yellow sedge at Malham Tarn, and all the specialities of the Craven limestone including alpine bortsia, baneberry, birdseye primrose and mountain pansy. Then there is the ancient woodland at Hawkswick, which I shall forever associate with the scent of lily of the valley, the green woods and meadows around Arncliffe, and lanes bordered by yellow minulus. The name Arncliffe literally means 'eagle's cliff'; were there once eagles, I wonder, soaring above the forbidding fells? There are other rarities of nature all over the area - purple saxifrage on Ingleborough and Pen-y-ghent, and alpine species of bistort, cinquefoil and penny-cress. Here, too, are many ancient trees, reminding me that bows were cut from old yews in that part of Yorkshire for the Battle of Flodden.

I have always been fascinated by butterflies ever since I thrilled at the sight of a small tortoiseshell on the wing in early March and became a butterfly-collecting schoolboy. The British butterflies are all so lovely in their different ways that I would be hard put to it to name a favourite. The orange-tip, the painted lady and the pretty, small copper would come close to the top of my list, but so too would the chalk-hill blue.

Normally a butterfly associated with Southern England, I used to see this lovely insect in some plenty on the Sussex downs, but it was always much easier to see than to catch. The male of the species is best described as silvery blue, sometimes very pale or tinged with green, whereas the female is sooty brown in colour. The undersides of both sexes consist of black spots ringed with white, and on the outer margin of the hind wings there are more black spots, edged outwardly with white and inwardly with orange. The butterfly is on the wing in July and August, and I have always felt it to represent the very essence of an English summer.

When I was a very small boy I was given a battered old book on British butterflies, from which my mother read extracts at bedtime. There are two passages from that book which caught my attention at the time and which have set my imagination working all my life. The first was that the magnificent purple emperor 'has been recorded as far north as Yorkshire', and the second was that 'nearly a hundred and fifty years ago a man recorded that he had seen chalk-hill blue butterflies literally swarming on a hillside between Settle and Bentham'.

Could it be, I often wondered as a butterfly-collecting schoolboy, that there were still purple emperors flying in oak woods south of Doncaster, and that somewhere in the magical countryside around Settle and upper Wharfedale, where eagles once flew, reindeer roamed and where lady's slipper orchids and yellow sedges flowered, that there might be a colony of chalk-hill blues surviving yet in a long-lost limestone world, undisturbed and forgotten?

In the years following my boyhood enthusiasm for collecting butterflies, I had occasionally in moments of daydreaming wondered whether there might just still be chalk-hill blues near Settle. But work and marriage and bringing up children had become my major preoccupation, and the thought had been all but erased from my memory when the subject arose, totally unexpectedly, during a routine conveyancing transaction I was undertaking about ten years ago. Tom Armitage was then fifty five years old. He had just taken early retirement from the civil service, for whom he had worked ever since leaving school. I had known him from boyhood, when he gave me some cricket and tennis coaching, and it was on a tennis court that our shared interest in British butterflies first came to light. An orange tip had flown across the court as I was about to serve, and we had both instictively stopped playing to watch the butterfly.

'So you're another entomologist', he said.

After we had finished playing tennis, he took me back to his home where he showed me his magnificent butterfly collection. Every British butterfly was represented in that collection, the specimens all immaculately mounted and displayed in neat columns. The first drawer contained the well-known garden butterflies - red admirals, peacocks, small tortoiseshells, painted ladies, and the large, small, and green-veined whites. The second contained woodland and hedgerow varieties, and the rest were full of blues, coppers, skippers and hairstreaks. There were two particularly fine drawers of the fritillaries - all brown, black, and spotted and splashed with silver.

After I had looked with schoolboy wonder at this fine collection, Tom showed me his library of butterfly books, particularly those concentrating on Yorkshire and of old records for the county.

I had completely forgotten all about Tom Armitage, his tennis and his interest in Yorkshire butterflies, when ten years ago he asked me to act for him in the purchase of his retirement cottage. I may have forgotten Tom, but he hadn't forgotten me.

'I haven't needed a solicitor for years', he said on the telephone. 'But a little bird told me that my old tennis partner had grown up and become a legal eagle. You will act for me, won't you?'

'Tom Armitage', I replied as I suddenly remembered him. 'Of course, I'll be delighted to act for you. Do you still play cricket and tennis?'

I realised I was speaking like an over-excited schoolboy rather than as a serious legal adviser.

'Now I'm retired, John, I'm going to spend my time doing the things I've always wanted to do. To start with, I'm going to find out for myself whether the Settle record is true or not.'

'The Settle record?' I said, repeating Tom's words.

'Don't you remember, John, we often used to talk about old Yorkshire butterfly records?'

'Oh, you're talking about butterflies, are you? You mean the old record of chalk-hill blues being seen somewhere between Settle and Bentham. Wasn't it supposed to link up with the records for North Lancashire and Westmorland? Nobody believes that now, do they?'

'That's right', replied Tom, ignoring my question. 'Grange and Silverdale in the west, Arnside and Beetham to the east and down to Settle in the south.'

'But they're all supposed to be wrong those records aren't they?' I said. 'Chalk-hill blues haven't been seen in any of those places for years, and if they ever were there, they disappeared years ago.'

'The Bermuda Triangle', mused Tom.

'Well', I replied, 'I remember reading an article by that learned entomologist Mr Wright who reckoned all the records were erroneous when he analysed them for the *Entomologist* magazine.'

'I'm not so sure', replied Tom.

I was about to ask him why this was when my secretary Clare came into my office, and it occurred to me that I should really be concentrating on the job in hand.

'Er, now about this cottage you're buying, Tom, when can you come and see me?'

The conveyancing transaction was duly completed, and I thought little more about our conversation until a year ago when one day towards the end of July I received a telephone call from him. He sounded excited.

20

'Eureka! I've found them, John.'

'Hello, Tom, how are you and what have you found?'

'Why coridon of course.' He used the butterfly's latin name with the instinct of a lifelong naturalist. 'Coridon - chalk-hill blues - scores of them. The Settle record. Its true, I've seen them, they've been there all the time.' He was almost breathless in his excitement.

'Are you pulling my leg?', I asked.

'Come and see for yourself, John. I want you to be my witness. I can't trust anyone else.'

I looked at my diary quickly for I felt as excited as he was. There were a lot of appointments written down, but there are times when a country solicitor must get his priorities right!

'I'll come with you tomorrow.'

'Right, John, eleven o'clock at my place and I'll take you there but you must promise not to tell anyone. It's our secret.'

I wasn't sure quite what to think as I made a solemn promise to Tom before putting the phone down and asking my long-suffering secretary Clare to explain to clients that their appointments had to be rearranged as 'Mr Francis had been called away on urgent business'.

Tom was an experienced and knowledgeable naturalist - of that there was no doubt - but could that old Settle record really be true? If it was, it would be an absolutely sensational discovery. Like me, Tom had long ago given up collecting and was now only interested in observing, photographing, conserving and recording Yorkshire butterflies. To discover a colony of chalk-hill blues in the county would be the crowning achievement of his retirement.

So it was that I met Tom at his cottage the next morning, and we set off in his car on the road to Settle. As we travelled we both thought it might be a wasted journey, for the weather was overcast and the dark clouds on the horizon threatened rain.

'We need some sunshine to bring out the butterflies', I remarked as we set off.

We talked little after that as we passed through all the well-loved villages on a road we both knew so well: Gargrave, Hellifield, Long Preston and finally Settle. The sun came out as we wended our way through the little town - which seemed a good omen - and I looked again in wonder at the magical and ancient landscape high above Giggleswick, with Ingleborough and Pen-y-ghent rising nearby where the lofty limestone scars above the road to Clapham mark the line of the Craven fault.

Tom suddenly stopped his car in a layby.

'Sorry about this John, but I must ask you to put on this blindfold. It's not that I don't trust you, but I made a decision when I made my discovery that I was not going to tell anyone in the world how to get to this place.'

I was disappointed but not in the least hurt or suprised by Tom's request, for I have learnt over many years that many naturalists become almost obsessively secretive about their discoveries for fear that others would discover and ruin them. I put on the blindfold and we continued on our way.

To be blindfolded is to enter a world of complete darkness and I quickly lost all sense of direction. The rest of the journey probably only lasted twenty minutes or so, but it seemed to go on forever.

Eventually I was aware that we had turned off the road and were motoring slowly down a bumpy track, along which we stopped three or four times for Tom to open and close gates.

At last the car stopped and Tom removed my blindfold.

'Let there be light', I thought to myself, and there was light.

I blinked as I stepped out of the car into brilliant sunshine. I had absolutely no idea where I was; there were no roads, houses, buildings or other landmarks by which I could get my bearings.

'It's about ten minutes' walk from here', said Tom.

I looked at the countryside around me. I was standing in the middle of an old-fashioned wildflower meadow of the kind that was common in the Dales up to fifty years ago, but of which there are nowadays precious few left. The meadow had not yet been cut for hay, and the sound and sight of a long-lost natural world was everywhere. The whole area teemed with all manner of bird and insect life, and the meadow flowers were a riot of colour.

'It's just a little further', said Tom, looking anxiously at some black clouds which had again appeared on the horizon. We walked to the end of the next flower meadow, where there was a steep limestone bank stretching up to some deciduous woodland.

'A naturalist's paradise', I thought to myself.

Even before I reached the bank I let out a cry of amazement as I saw literally dozens of blue butterflies frolicking in the sunshine, along with small coppers and skippers.

As I got close to the butterflies I realised that they were just common blues flying round some birdsfoot trefoil.

'They're only common blues', I said to Tom, barely able to conceal my disappointment.

'Yes, there are plenty of common blues here as well', he replied. 'But just look a bit closer.'

I followed Tom's suggestion, and within seconds I spotted among the bright common blues a number of pale silver-blue butterflies which I immediately recognised as chalk-hills.

Tom could not help laughing out loud as I did a double take which would have graced the stage of my local amateur dramatic society. I sat on the bank, and gazed in sheer wonder and amazement.

'So, they are here after all. This is a story to tell - but who will believe us. Where's our proof? Have you brought a camera, Tom?'

As I spoke the sun disappeared behind the black clouds which had rapidly moved from the horizon to almost directly overhead. By the time Tom had got his camera out of the car, it was too late. It had started raining, and as if by the wave of a conjuror's wand the hundreds of butterflies had disappeared.

'I don't think we'll see any more butterflies today, Tom', I said as we got into the car. Heavy rain swept over the flower meadows and the limestone hill.

'It doesn't matter now', replied Tom. 'You've seen them and you are my witness that I was telling you the truth. I'm a happy man now.'

Tom asked me to put my blindfold back on until we were back in Settle, and after a quick cup of tea back at Tom's house I made my excuses, as our butterfly expedition had seriously cut short my working day.

I had planned to phone Tom the next morning to discuss how or indeed whether we should publicise our discovery. Instead I received a phone call from his neighbour and friend Jock Fornham. As a solicitor I am used to hearing bad news, but what Jock had to tell me came as a considerable shock. Tom was dead, having suffered a massive coronary during the night. It was hard for me to take this in. Had it only been yesterday that we were both walking in a long-lost limestone world of chalk-hill blues and pre-glacial flora?

I went straight round to Tom's cottage, and found his nature diary lying open on his desk. His last entry, written I guess only minutes before his death, read:

'Today my solicitor was a witness to my discovery of a thriving colony of chalk-hill blue butterflies at a certain place in Yorkshire, the culmination of years of searching. A red letter day indeed and perhaps the happiest of my life.'

My friend's death had come as a tremendous shock, but as I reflected afterwards, he could not have written the script for it better if he had tried. It was, I thought, rather similar to the fisherman who expired immediately after landing the biggest salmon he had ever caught in his life, or the golfer who dropped dead after scoring his first hole in one.

Some weeks later I showed Tom's diary to the eminent Yorkshire naturalist, Professor Henry Reynard.

'There's a mistake here isn't there Mr Francis?', he said. 'I know Tom was a good butterfly man but his mind must have been going at the end. There's that old Settle record I know, but what sort of a person would believe that there are any chalk-hill blues in Yorkshire these days?'

I looked straight at him as I replied quickly.

'A person like me, professor, a person like me.'

'Come along, Mr Francis, pull the other one', said the professor, laughing as he spoke.

I waited a few seconds before replying.

'I know, professor, for I have seen them.'

Auntie Dot

A solicitor never knows quite what to expect when he meets a new client for the first time.

There have been quite a few meetings over the years which have been unforgettable, none more so than the one which took place on a lovely summer's day twenty-odd years ago when I travelled up the dale from Denley to the rather isolated village of East Stonebeck, passing over the lonely moors which my old friend and country doctor James Meredith always called 'Indian Country'. Little did I suspect that I was about to meet and become firm friends with one of the great characters of my practising life.

I made this journey to meet a certain Miss Dorothy Lacey-Smith to discuss a small problem concerning her boundary fences and to advise her on a new will she wished to make. I was to learn years later that the reason she had asked me to be her solicitor was that she had heard from someone in the village that I had played a decent game of tennis the last time I turned out for Denley against East Stonebeck. It's as good a way of choosing a solicitor as any other, I suppose.

I had to stop in the village to ask for directions to the house.

'Miss Lacey-Smith?', said a good-natured villager. 'She lives on her own in that big house at the end of the main street; we all call her Auntie Dot.'

A sprightly lady of about seventy opened the door of the large rambling, stone-built house to which I had been directed. She had a face which was full of character and individuality, a rosy complexion, smiling blue eyes, curls of silky white hair and she wore what was even then a rather old-fashioned tweed suit. I could see immediately why the whole village knew and loved her as 'Auntie Dot', for her whole being exuded warmth, energy and kindness.

'How do you do Mr Francis, do come in, it's so kind of you to come all this way to see me', she said as she walked briskly along the hall and into her drawing room.

As I walked down the hall, I stopped dead in my tracks as I heard a voice from the drawing room say in a broad Yorkshire accent:

'Bugger off, bugger off.'

I peeped rather cautiously around the drawing room door, and was puzzled to see only Auntie Dot standing there.

'Don't take any notice of Peregrine', she said with a laugh, as she pointed to her pretty mynah bird in a cage on the sideboard.

As we started to talk business our conversation was constantly interrupted by Peregrine. He did not say 'pieces of eight', but he did squawk 'bugger off' again and 'a'd best put t' taties on', and then almost immediately and unaccountably switched from broad Yorkshire to cut-glass English with a 'not today thank you', 'how do you do' and 'so very kind'.

It transpired that Auntie Dot employed a woman from the village who came in to help her with cleaning and cooking. Mrs Slater was a kindly Yorkshire woman, but unlike her employer was rather prone to using bad language in the best Anglo-Saxon tradition.

So when salesmen came to the door, Auntie Dot would say in the nicest possible way 'not today thank you', whereas Mrs Slater would simply tell them to 'bugger off'. Peregrine had obviously listened carefully both to his mistress and her domestic help, and had memorised their favourite phrases - which now came out at random.

I had known a little about Auntie Dot before our first meeting, for her reputation was by no means confined to her own village. The entire population of East Stonebeck had been stunned in 1950 when

Colonel and Mrs Ronald Lacey-Smith were killed in a car crash. There had been Lacey-Smiths in the village for generations, and the tragic accident meant that there was only one survivor - their daughter Dorothy.

At the time of her parents' death she was unmarried, and she was to remain in that state for the rest of her life. It was said that she had fallen in love only once - with an army officer whose wife was in a mental hospital - but that her sense of honour had compelled her to end the relationship. There had never been anyone else.

She had been a tremendously active woman all her life. At school and university her first-class brain was complemented by her outstanding prowess on the sports field. She was an outstanding tennis player, golfer, horsewoman and swimmer.

Her parents had left her comfortably off, and she decided to dedicate herself to the village in the way they always did when they were alive. She became headmistress of the village school, and there was hardly an organisation in the area with which she was not associated: the church, the Womens Institute, St Johns Ambulance, the tennis club, the annual village fête and many more benefited from her ability and enthusiasm. She was a dedicated voluntary social worker, a Barnado's Auntie, and a regular visitor of prisons and hospitals. Above all, she loved children. The fact that she had no children of her own did not appear to sadden her greatly.

'You see, my dear, they are all my children', she once said, speaking of the pupils at her village school.

Miss Dorothy Lacey-Smith rapidly became known to everyone in the village as 'Auntie Dot', for she was indeed everyone's favourite aunt. Her large rambling house and garden were the village children's special playground.

It struck me at our first meeting that she must have been strikingly beautiful in her day for she still looked lovely, rather in the style of Dame Anna Neagle or Greer Garson: quintessentially English and with that rather posh accent one always associates with ladies of her period and class.

Following our rather strange first meeting, Auntie Dot and I became firm friends and I always looked forward to my visits to East Stonebeck. The more I came to know about her, the more my admiration for her grew. I quickly learnt that she was still playing tennis, swimming twice a week and having the occasional ride, and when she was not doing any of these things she was walking in the country, playing a round of golf or enjoying a rubber of bridge with her friends.

I was soon to learn too that she was an indefatigable worker for the Conservative party, God, Queen and Country; her hero was Sir Winston Churchill. A large portrait of him adorned her drawing room. She read all his books and knew his speeches by heart. She never wavered from her lifelong beliefs.

'I wish I was sure about everything as you are', I remember once saying to her.

Yet she was far from being a typical woman Conservative of the older generation, for she was very much her own person, different, highly individual and a real character.

I loved her sense of humour, and laughed out loud the time she recounted her first visit to her new doctor following the death of old Doctor Jameson, who had been a friend of her father and had looked after her family for years.

'Went down to see my new doctor this morning, John. Can't say that I liked him very much actually. Very earnest. One of these fitness fanatics. No sense of fun. Not my type at all, I'm afraid.

"Now Dorothy ...", he had begun.

I didn't like his patronising manner or calling me by my christian name on our very first meeting.

"Do you smoke?" he asked me.

"Yes, doctor", I replied, without guilt or hesitation. "I've smoked twenty a day for over fifty years. It's leaving it a bit late to give them up now, don't you think? Anyway, they've seen me through some difficult times and I wouldn't give them up now."

"I see", replied the doctor in a tone of voice which did not trouble to conceal his obvious disapproval.

"Do you drink?", was the next question.

29

"Yes I jolly well do, doctor. I wouldn't be without my glass of sherry before lunch and I love a couple of gins of an evening."

Well, John, the young doctor looked at me even more disapprovingly. I decided to speak before he could.

"Doctor Firth, I've cheerfully admitted to smoking and drinking, so I'd better anticipate your next question. No, doctor, I don't go with men anymore."

Do you know, John, there wasn't a flicker of a smile on his face. He thought I wasn't taking him seriously enough.'

Auntie Dot had told the truth when she had described herself as a moderate smoker, but she wasn't entirely honest in claiming her evening drinking was always confined to a couple of gins. Mrs Slater confided to me on more than one occasion that one of these days she might find her employer 'flat on t' floor'.

Whenever I think of Auntie Dot, I see her in my mind's eye through a haze of cigarette smoke, pouring her third - or was it her fourth? - gin and saying:

'Sorry, John, I couldn't wait. I've already opened the bar.'

Not that I found her on her own very often when I called, for there always seemed to be friends, acquaintances, relations, former pupils and villagers there, sometimes for advice and other times just for the pleasure of her company. Everyone, it seemed, felt better just for seeing her.

That was how I always felt too. Like many women, she talked a lot but, in her case, the talk was always worth hearing. She had her foibles and prejudices of course, and the one which I particularly associate with her was the importance she always attached to buying British. She once scolded me for not knowing whether my new briefcase had been made in this country, and I am quite convinced that I would have lost her as a client had I turned up to see her in a Japanese car.

She had no scruples whatsoever about demanding an interview with local shop managers to ask why, for instance, there was only Danish bacon on their shelves.

'And it worked', she told me triumphantly. 'On my next visit there was prime British bacon - just as there should be, my dear.'

Although a lady of strong moral principles, she showed her sypathetic and tolerant nature when confronted by the failing of an individual. She hated the sin but loved the sinner. She regularly babysat for single mothers and acted as their own mothers.

There was an occasion which she often recalled with amusement. She was working for the Conservatives one general election, and her job was to take a number of people by car to the polling station from a list supplied to her by the Committee.

'It really was the worst job they could have given me, my dear. I'm afraid I didn't do very well at all. They gave me six names and addresses. The first two were out, the third and fourth had already voted, and the fifth was in bed with flu. The sixth person on the list was a lady who, how shall I put it, well, my dear, she wasn't fully in possession of her mental faculties.

"Oh, I'm so pleased to see you", she greeted me. "I've been looking forward to our trip so much."

Well, John, it soon came out that the old dear imagined that someone from the social services was coming to take her for a day out around the Dales.'

The voluntary social worker in Auntie Dot had immediately taken over as all political thoughts and considerations were cast to the wind.

'Well, John, I took her out in my car, and we went around the Dales, finishing up at Bolton Abbey for tea. I did most of the talking. She just kept saying "Lovely, lovely, how lovely" all the time. I just remembered in time to take her to the polling station on the way home, and when we stopped the car outside it, she said "What are we doing here? I thought you were just taking me out for tea."

Actually, John, the polling clerk looked rather sharply at me as I led her firmly by the arm to the booth, repeating the word "Conservative" in her ear rather loudly. I rather think she might have voted Labour. Anyway, John, she had a jolly nice tea.'

When Auntie Dot reached her ninetieth birthday she was still going strong. She had given up golf, but was still walking two miles every day and enjoying her weekly swim. She was still fond of a smoke and a drink, too, as I found one morning just before her birthday when, after the usual greeting from her newest mynah bird, I was offered a gin and tonic.

'You're late again John, I'm already on my third gin', she said reproachfully.

'Bugger off, bugger off', said the mynah bird again as I toasted her.

'Really, Algernon - manners, manners', said Auntie Dot.

I smiled as I reflected that all the mynah birds she had had over the years were always given aristocratic names - Peregrine and Algernon were her favourites - and all of them spoke in a distinctly unaristocratic way.

As I sat down, she started talking about her neighbours. She didn't pull any punches.

'Muriel Fogarty - it's high time she pulled her socks up and made an effort.' This struck me as a rather severe comment as I knew Muriel to be at least eighty-five years old.

'And as for Marjorie Tyler', she continued, 'you know John, she's become awfully forgetful lately.' This, I thought, was rather good coming from a nonagenarian about an octogenarian.

'I do wish Elizabeth and Dick wouldn't keep calling to see if I'm alright. They're in and out and up and down like yo-yos. Fuss, fuss, fuss. Of course I'm alright. I've never felt better in my life. I'll live to be a hundred - you jolly well see if I don't.'

I believed her.

As the months and years passed, it began to look as if her promise might be fulfilled. It is true that she slowed down a little and became rather deaf, but she was otherwise in full possession of her faculties. Some of the villagers, however, became increasingly worried about her advancing age. After a sneak thief had stolen some money which Auntie Dot had left in the kitchen - she always left her home unlocked - one of them contacted the social services, who then sent someone to see her.

Debbie Reynolds was twenty-three years old - Auntie Dot's junior by nearly seventy years, She had learnt a lot of theory at college, but had still much to learn in the university of life.

She came through the unlocked door, but before she could speak she was greeted with the usual 'Bugger off, bugger off' from Peregrine - or was it Algernon? Auntie Dot was much too kind to give Debbie the same advice, but quickly made it clear that she was quite alright on her own and didn't need any help from social services, 'thank you very much, dear'.

Debbie saw through the cigarette smoke that the house was clean and tidy, and there was certainly no evidence of neglect.

'You'll stay for a cup of coffee, won't you my dear?', said Dot in her usual, hospitable way.

'I really should be going - I just wanted to make sure you were alright...well, if you insist', replied Debbie.

There was something about the young woman's demeanour which revealed to Dot from a lifetime of experience that the social worker was herself far from alright.

As they drank their coffee and started talking, Dot's suspicion that Debbie had problems proved to be fully justified.

'There's something the matter isn't there, my dear?', Dot said after some time. 'Don't tell me about it if you don't want to.'

Now, although Dot had never had any children of her own, she had taught generations of them and always got on particularly well with young people. She had a way of crossing the generation gap, making them feel comfortable and at ease talking to her.

'I've made such a mess of my life', sobbed Debbie.

'It can't be that much of a mess, my dear', replied Dot. 'It's never as bad as you think.'

Two hours later Debbie took her leave of Auntie Dot, her tangled love-life seemingly sorted out.

'I think *she* was sent to help *me*', said Auntie Dot with a smile when she told me all about Debbie's visit.

The social services department did not trouble her again, nor did they need to, because despite her great age she retained all her interests and enthusiasm, her love of life and of people. Most important of all, she kept her health. In fact she often boasted that she had never been to hospital in her life except to visit and comfort others staying there, and she had an absolute horror of doctors and pills.

For all the world Auntie Dot could probably have gone on living on her own almost indefinitely, had it not been for the fact that she lived in such a large house. Even though a man from the village came to do the garden and old Mrs Slater came every day to help in the house, it seemed ridiculous for an old lady to live on her own in such a place. Yet it was the only home she had ever known. For her to leave it, I felt, would be certain death.

Her friends in the village became increasingly concerned for her. They were not so much worried about her ability to cope on her own - for she could still look after herself pretty well - but they realised just how vulnerable she had become to burglary.

These fears were realised one day when a young man knocked at the door, told her his car had broken down and asked to use the telephone. Whilst she was showing him to the phone, his accomplice came in and searched the house whilst Dot's back was turned.

It was some time later that she discovered some cash and silver were missing. The two youths must have told their friends, for after that Dot's home was burgled three times in six months.

The villagers were all increasingly worried, but Dot was philosophical.

'I can't take any of these things with me', she told me one day.

'It's you they're worried about', I replied. 'The next time you might be hurt.'

On her ninety-fifth birthday, a party was held at her house. Dot was happy, but it was a happiness tinged with sadness, for she knew that her friends were right and that she could not go on living alone in such a large house. Yet, as she told me quietly before the cutting of the cake, the prospect of living in an old folk's home, the loss of independence and dependence on others were things she could hardly bear to face.

'I never could see you in an old peoples' home', I said to her.

'I don't think you will, my dear', she replied.

In a gracious and moving speech after her toast had been proposed, Auntie Dot seemed to be acknowledging that she might have to move on. As she looked at the friendly faces of her many friends and at her lounge, full as always of books and flowers and children's drawings, she said:

'I've decided that I've lived here long enough. You've all been so very kind.'

'So very kind', repeated Algernon - or was it Peregrine?

The next day, the kindly, faithful but now rather elderly Mrs Slater called to do the housework as usual, and found Auntie Dot dead in her favourite armchair.

'So peaceful, like', as she told the villagers later.

On the table next to the armchair was a packet of cigarettes, an empty glass which I guess had contained her last gin and tonic, and a book of Churchill's speeches. She had died at a time and in a way she would have wished. There would be no old folk's home for her. She had instead reached the broad sunlit uplands of which her hero once so movingly spoke.

Edgar's Law

I have said before that farmers are a law unto themselves, and are as a group quite different from the rest of my clients.

I have had the privilege of knowing and advising many over the years - arable farmers, pig men, dairy men and those with old-fashioned mixed farms - but if I had to choose my favourite kind of farmer, the type I most respect and admire, I think it would have to be that very special and presently endangered species - the Dales hill-sheep farmer.

Edgar Fearn is such a man and for him, like his father and grandfather before him, the moors and the fells represent a very ancient way of life. Whenever I go to see him in winter, either for business or pleasure, and walk with him on the moorland part of his farm, I know exactly what the author of Deuteronomy meant when he wrote of 'a howling wilderness'.

It is an illusion for some to believe that such men spend a happy life walking their dogs among beautiful scenery inbetween collecting their sheep subsidies. In truth it is a very hard life indeed, and one in which few are likely to succeed unless they have been literally born to it or at any rate worked at it for a very long time.

As Edgar once put it to me:

'Up 'ere, its not like t' vale o' York or t' Garden of Eden, tha knows.'

The income of hill-sheep farmers is decidedly meagre, and it has always struck me that the constant round of gathering, dipping, clipping, tupping, winter feeding and spring lambing must be one of the toughest and exhausting for anyone to undertake.

Edgar's main living comes from selling the wool from his sheep and from rearing and selling his stock, but in recent years he would not have survived without keeping a small herd of cows on the lowland part of his farm and his wife Joan making her contribution by taking in visitors for bed and breakfast during the summer months.

But Edgar has always been a sheep man through and through. A fine upstanding man with a handsome, weather-beaten face, I shall always picture him out on the moors carrying a stout walking stick 'among t' sheep' and at all times accompanied by his ever-faithful sheepdog Jock.

Edgar knows his part of the Dales like the back of his hand, and of course he knows all his sheep individually by their gait, looks and markings.

Like all shepherds through the ages, he is much better at forecasting the weather than the professional pundits.

'There's a snow wind comin'', he once said to me.

I truly believed he could feel the weather in his bones as he sniffed the air and seemed to sense that the weather vane on the distant village church spire was already turning north.

His sheep are Swaledales which, like Teeswater, Masham, Wensleydale and Dalesbred, are noted for their hardiness and come from the indigenous stock of the fells. Hill sheep have to be hardy, for in winter the weather can be very bleak indeed. Their ability to survive in deep snow is legendary. At such times, Edgar and his fellow shepherds have to prod the snow with a big stick whilst their dogs sniff for any sheep presence. Edgar once explained to me that if sheep can stay on their feet in such conditions they can survive for a very long time - sometimes even eating their own wool to do so - but if they couldn't manage to stay on their feet it would be 'all ovver wi' 'em'.

Whenever I visit Edgar it is difficult to keep him off his favourite subject for long, and he oftens contrasts the difficulties of keeping moorland as opposed to lowland sheep. It is a good job that I know a little about the subject, for sheep talk is a language all of its own. I

know for instance from the many farm sales I have handled over the years that moor sheep are called 'heughed sheep', and because they generally stay on their own territory they are valued and sold with the farm. But Edgar's talk always goes far beyond 'heughed sheep'.

'Aye, Mr Francis, they're an ockard lot, an' there's allus a few on 'em as are reight ockard. Tha's git tae let 'em know who's t' boss or t' beggars'll be t' boss o' thee.'

His talk is always peppered with references to yows (ewes), tups (rams), wethers (castrated males) and gimmers (virgin ewes). He frequently refers to the moorland country over which his sheep roam in a language of its own. It is some years since I had to ask him what he meant by 'spriggets an' cowling', the first being the fresh growth and the second referring to the burnt stalks of heather.

Edgar is one of a dwindling band of farmers who still use the old system of counting sheep - a tradition which goes back to the Celts.

I once watched him as he counted the first five.

'Yan, tean, tither, mither, pip', he called out. 'Aye, Mr Francis', he said. 'Ah still counts 'em like me father an' gran'father afore me.'

He was an expert when it came to moorland sheep.

'They're more like wild sheep is that lot', he once said to me. 'They'll tek what they can, given t' chance. It's oft t' ockard uns as gives t' best and biggest lambs. It's 'ard tae reckon t' job up many a time.'

Edgar's world of sheep, grey-stone walls, green pastures and heather moorland is centred on his farmhouse set in the midst of the Dales National Park, and the story I have to tell is about his particular skill in overcoming the difficulties which arise from living in such a place.

Now there are many beautiful places in England but I have to say, being completely objective and unbiased of course, that our own Yorkshire Dales are very hard to beat.

This country of fells and dales is situated in the heart of the Pennine chain and covers more than a thousand square miles, part of which has been classed as one of England's National Parks. Each dale is different in character: Swaledale, wild and rugged; Wensleydale, broad and beautiful; Nidderdale, softer and more pastoral; Wharfedale, green and limestone-scarred at its top end; and many more, each with their own particular characteristics and attractions.

Nobody knows better than Edgar that one of the most misleading names or titles ever to be given to an area of countryside is a 'National Park'. To the dismay of Edgar, his fellow farmers and others who happen to live in such an area, many members of the general public, especially those who live in towns and cities, take this title at face value. They regard it as a place where they can go where they like, picnic where they please and generally treat it as if it was their own.

What they completely fail to understand or appreciate is that virtually all of the land and property within a National Park is, in fact, privately owned. Consequently, members of the general public have no greater rights within its boundaries than they would over anywhere else.

Visitors do not realise that the countryside they come to admire is there because of the work of farmers and landowners whose living depends on it. Perversely, many regard these guardians of our heritage as a threat. It is in truth a landscape which is very much man-made and managed, the heather moorland in particular being the result of a combination of grouse shooting, sheep grazing and a carefully-planned programme in which the heather is burnt off at regular intervals to allow new growth. It is an environment in which all manner of bird and insect life can flourish. It is the home not just of the red grouse but also of the golden plover, the curlew and the snipe.

Lambing time is, of course, the most critical period in any sheep farmer's year. Lambs, which are prone to all kinds of diseases, are often said by farmers to try their hardest to die. Edgar has often remarked to me that he has 'all on' to avoid losses he cannot afford, without losing more through the actions of visitors and their dogs. This is just one of the many problems he has to face in living right in the middle of the National Park.

Now Edgar has never had any objection to the majority of walkers and visitors who keep to the public footpaths and generally show a respect for the countryside; indeed he always makes a point of welcoming such people, often stopping work to chat to them, and point out features of interest in the surrounding countryside, particular fauna and flora, or special things to look out for.

What, however, has always made Edgar's life merry hell at times is the arrogant and inconsiderate attitudes of an irresponsible minority. The problems they cause are many and various. The chief change in the National Park is that of visitors ruining the very places they come to enjoy - wild areas which have existed for hundreds of years, looked after by farmers and countrymen long before the coming of car-borne tourists.

Among the many problems Edgar and his fellow farmers have to face are gates left open, litter left everywhere, dogs roaming off the lead, vandalism to farm buildings, walls broken down and noise from transistor radios.

They face enough problems of their own without those caused by tourists. Quite apart from the difficulties in making a living in a rough terrain, they, who have been guardians of the landscape for generations, have become increasingly angry and demoralised by petty planning restrictions imposed by planning officers enforcing over-restrictive regulations.

So Edgar was weary of asking ramblers with dogs to keep them on a lead, he was tired of picking up cigarette packets, cans and other tourist debris, he was fed up with having to remove old tyres and washing machines dumped on his land, and he was absolutely furious when he had spent many hours separating sheep, only to find that visitors leaving a gate open had let them all become mixed up again within a few minutes.

I first gained an insight into Edgar's methods of dealing with problems caused by tourists when he explained how he resolved his difficulties with one particular family who frequently came to picnic, and always chose to do so in the meadow just beyond his farmhouse.

Eddie and Karen, together with their numerous small children and assorted relatives, were not welcome to Edgar, for they always made a lot of noise, allowed their dogs to stray, tended to drink rather too much alcohol and left a great deal of litter. Edgar had on several occasions pointed out to them that they were on private property and it would have been courteous to have asked his permission to be there. It was a dialogue with the deaf - and he always got the same answer.

'What's it to do wi' you? It's public land is this. There's a big sign back down t' road that says "National Park". It's public property we're on, so it's nowt to do wi' you.'

'That's not reight', replied Edgar quietly. 'It *is* summat to do wi' me, 'cos it's my land tha's landed on and them's my sheep thy dog were chasin'. An' who dus tha reckon 'as tae pick up all t' rubbish tha leaves 'ere?'

This gentle, reasoned approach got Edgar nowhere, and good few choice expletives followed him as he set off back to his farmhouse.

After he had suffered further visits and further insults from Eddie, Karen and their menagerie, Edgar eventually hit upon an idea. One day he followed Eddie's car all the way to the house in Leeds where he and his family lived. Edgar couldn't help noticing that, whilst many of the houses on the estate were very well-maintained, Eddie and Karen's house looked shabby and uncared for, and the garden was a complete wilderness. Edgar had often wondered how those who left litter on his land treated their own property. Now he knew. All this he had observed from a safe distance to make sure that he had not been spotted. The next Sunday, Edgar gathered together his own family and the neighbouring farmers' families who had also suffered. They all piled into a couple of old Land Rovers, crammed in their children and a couple of dogs, and set off.

Nobody was at home when they eventually arrived at Eddie and Karen's place, and they proceeded to set out a large picnic on the hayfield which passed for a lawn in the back garden.

'Aye, Mr Francis', related Edgar, 'when that lot came back they were fair capp'd, ah'll tell thee, when they set eyes on us all camped out on their back lawn.'

I chuckled loud and long as Edgar concluded this delightful tale, visualising the expressions on Eddie and Karen's faces being a mixture of surprise, disbelief and anger as they saw the large party of Dalesfolk picnicking on their back 'lawn', and as they eventually realised what was going on.

'Aye, there's more than one way o' skinnin' a cat', chuckled Edgar.

After the 'Dalesfolk's picnic' he never suffered from the same problem again - not, at any rate, from Eddie and Karen.

I noted how Edgar had achieved this result without undue unpleasantness, violence or litigation, and I was impressed. It is, however, the story of the wall stones for which I shall always remember Edgar, for it perhaps best illustrates his unique methods in handling problems caused by tourists.

One day, Edgar had been absolutely astounded to find a man and woman - whom he subsequently learnt were called Richard and Christine Smith - coolly helping themselves to stones from one of his walls which adjoined the only road in the area. He presumed they were taking them for their garden rockery - his presumption turned out to be correct.

Edgar was too far away to stop them, and by the time he got anywhere near they had loaded the stones into the back of their large estate car. He noticed, too, that as a result of their actions a section of the wall had collapsed completely.

He cursed silently to himself as he raced back to his farmhouse, got into his Land Rover and followed in pursuit. It was a long journey before Edgar eventually drew up outside Richard and Christine's neat suburban house on the outskirts of Leeds. He noticed that the garden was completely different to Eddie and Karen's. It was tidy to the point of fussiness: the lawns were manicured, there was a small lily-pond in the middle with gnomes fishing, and he guessed there was probably a chiming doorbell to the house as well. He also noticed that a fresh rockery had been made ready, waiting only for the addition of some strategically-placed stones.

'Tha's gitten summat as dusn't belong to thee, Ah reckons', said Edgar as Richard and Christine finished unloading the stones from the back of their car. They both looked up in surprise, and it was Richard who spoke first.

'Just who are you and what the hell are you talking about?'

Edgar said nothing, merely pointing to the stones which lay next to the rockery.

At this point Christine joined in the argument.

'They're not yours, they're from the National Park. Anyway there's miles and miles of walls - who's going to miss a few stones for our rockery?'

'That's just wheer tha's mistaken, missus', replied Edgar. 'Them stones is mine. Ah've followed thee all t' way from my place, an' them stones is off o' one o' my walls. What dus tha reckon would 'appen if t' rest o' t' population were tae tek t' same attitude? Why missus, Ah'll tell thee - there'd be nowt left o' my walls, an' wheer dus tha reckon t' sheep would be gittin' tae then? Nay, missus, them stones 'aven't bin put theer tae be tekken' for mekkin' rockeries, tha knows.'

Richard and Christine were silent for a minute. They were at first defensive and then became abusive.

'Na then', said Edgar. 'Ah reckons t' time 'as cum tae put them stones in t' back o' my Land Rovver, an' we can all tek 'em an' put 'em back wheer they belong.'

'But they're for our rockery', shouted Christine. 'Anyway, how do we know they're yours?'

'It's up to thee', replied Edgar, with a shrug of his shoulders, 'but if tha's not gitten' t' Land Rovver loaded wi' them stones in t' next five minutes, Ah reckon this'll be a police job.' Richard and Christine both suddenly looked worried.

'Is that what tha wants?', Edgar went on, 'tae be charged with theft, like?'

'Charged with theft!', repeated Richard angrily. 'Don't be so ridiculous. How could it be theft? Those stones have come from the National Park.'

'That dusn't mean it's public property', replied Edgar. 'If it were, like, any beggar could go in theer an' tek what 'e wanted.'

'Oh, just let the man take the wretched stones', said Christine, who by this time was getting heartily fed up with the whole business.

Neither she nor her husband had given any thought at all to the fact that Edgar would have to spend valuable time unloading the stones and repairing the damaged section of wall himself. But he had another surprise in store for them.

'If tha wants tae stop this frae bein' a police job', he said quietly but firmly, 'Ah'll need t' pair o' thee tae cum back to t' farm an' 'elp wi' t' wallin'. Aye, an' tha'll need a decent pair o' gloves for t' job.'

'You can't be serious', said Richard.

'We're not going all that way back', said Christine.

'Reight, well it looks like a job for t' police then.'

Suddenly daunted at the prospect of their neighbours seeing the police arriving at their house, Richard and Christine looked at each other and came to the same conclusion. It was the husband who spoke for both.

'Oh, all right then. I hope it's not going to take long.'

They drove in convoy back to the Dales and unloaded the stones. Edgar pointed out to them the section of wall which had collapsed as a result of their actions. He then set about explaining to them the rudiments of drystone walling:

'Tae start wi", t' footings must be reight an' then it'll not tek any fault. Then t' courses must be even - one ovver two an' two ovver three tae cross t' joints. Tha wants tae start at t' bottom about two foot six wide an' taper up tae about a foot, wi' three rows o' throughs in it.'

Richard and Christine were in all honesty not much the wiser for this explanation, but they soon moved from theory to practice.

Edgar sent the unknowing couple to the other side of the wall and set them to work. At the same he time explained that the idea is to build in effect a double wall joined with wide stones called 'throughs' packed in the middle with small pieces of stone called 'fillings', which ideally should be put in one at a time not just thrown in.

And Edgar made them put them in, not throw them.

At this stage, Richard and Christine noticed that Edgar never put down a stone once he had picked it up, whereas they were constantly struggling to find ones of the right shape and size. They were learning that the ancient craft of dry stonewalling needs a good pair of hands and a keen eye. Good walling, as any Dalesman knows, is mainly done by 'reckovee' - the 'reckoning of the eye'.

To their surprise Richard and Christine gradually found themselves absorbed in the work, and eventually, with Edgar's encouragement and help, the section of wall had been rebuilt. Edgar ran his eye along the top to make sure it was level. He liked the 'throughs' to project a bit to strengthen the walls and to stop sheep jumping them. He stood back from it and, knowing that a decent bit of walling will last a hundred years, said quietly, 'Na then, it'll be standin' theer long after we've all bin dead and buried.'

By this time, Richard and Christine's attitude had undergone a remarkable transformation. In the first place they had felt angry and then guilty; secondly they had witnessed at first hand the work and skill needed in drystone walling, and they felt humble; finally, and most surprising of all, they had actually found themselves enjoying the physical work in repairing the wall and feeling the satisfaction to be gained in a job well done.

'They've bin back a time or two since', said Edgar to me the last time I went to see him. 'Not tae tek any more stones for t' rockery, but to 'elp me wi' one or two sections o' wallin' that needed doin' on yon moorside.'

Edgar smiled at me as he ended his story.

'Aye, Mr Francis, they're jus' like sheep is folks. There's a few leaders, but Ah reckons t' majority are nobbut followers - they'll not stray far on their own, they need to be wi' a flock - an' then there's allus a few ockard beggars that'll do what they like, an' to start wi' there's no 'oldin' 'em. Sheep and folks - it's t' ockard uns as 'ave to be brought into line, Ah reckons.'

46

'Capstan Carter'

Thomas Frederick Samuel Carter, to give him his full name, was one of the great characters of my boyhood.

He and his wife Gladys ran a smallholding just outside Denley, and it was one of those places which was always a magnet for children. We boys used to meet there after school, at weekends or during holidays to play cricket in his yard, help with jobs round the farm, or just to play. Perhaps because they had no children of their own, they compensated by christening Stocks Farm 'Liberty Hall'. The word somehow got round that children were welcome there, and to my knowledge no one needed a second invitation.

One of the main reasons for the attraction of 'Liberty Hall' was Mr Carter's home-made ice-cream, which he made both winter and summer alike. Gladys did all the cooking and just about everything else, but the ice-cream was her husband's domain, his pride and his joy.

'It's a poor belly that can't warm an ice-cream', he would say as he dolloped out huge cornets.

But he wasn't too popular with our parents when these were eaten just before we came home for the evening meal!

Now Mr Carter was not a man who would nowadays be described as politically correct. For a start he spent as much time at the Denley

Heifer as he did on his smallholding. He was also a chain smoker, not just of ordinary cigarettes but of Capstan Full Strength - hence his nickname of 'Capstan Carter'. He even smoked when he was playing cricket with us in the farmyard. He acted as umpire, and when there was a loud appeal for leg before wicket, we often had to wait an agonising time for the decision whilst his coughing fits had subsided, and the thick clouds of smoke cleared from around him.

He had what might be politely described as a traditional view of women - he gave the orders, but like all good wives Gladys had a way of getting round him.

So he liked a drink, he liked a smoke and his political opinions were someway to the right of Genghis Khan. Hanging, flogging and castration were some of the milder penalties he advocated for criminals, and as for foreigners, well, he reckoned that anyone south of Doncaster was suspect, only that wasn't the adjective he used.

For all this, however, 'Capstan Carter' was one of the most hospitable of men and the most interesting of characters. I think it was Norman Douglas who first observed that 'the ideal citizen is not the ideal man'. How perceptive of him and how very true. So in the schoolboy slang of my day he was 'wizard' and it was always 'a rotten swiz' when it was time to leave. What country schoolboy would want to leave a place where it was one long holiday, playing cricket, fishing, ferreting for rabbits with him, listening to his yarns about cattle rustling in days of yore - and all this against a background of limitless ice-cream washed down with dandelion and burdock. Those halcyon days passed, of course, and we boys grew up and went away to school and then university becoming more or less respectable citizens.

By the time I had qualified as a solicitor I hadn't seen 'Capstan Carter' for some years, and had almost forgotten about him. The years passed in building up my practice until I was asked by an old friend Joe Standwick at Denley cattle market:

'Had you heard that "Capstan" and Gladys have had to sell Stocks Farm?'

'No', I said, as I remembered my happy schoolboy days there. 'I don't think I will ever get used to the idea of them not being there.

48

Where are they now? I'd like to call in for a chat sometime and see how they're getting on.'

'They've moved into a cottage - t' old gamekeeper's cottage t' other side o' Denley Moor.'

'How are they keeping these days?', I asked.

'Well, it's a bit on a sad do, Ah reckons. T' old man's none sae bad but 'is missus is strugglin' wi' rheumatics, tha knows.'

A couple of weeks later I happened to be in their neck of the woods and decided to call in and see them.

'It's John Francis', I said. 'Do you remember me - my friends and I were always round at Stocks Farm playing cricket and driving the tractor and chasing rabbits.'

'Course Ah remembers', said 'Capstan', drawing heavily on what must have been the umpteenth cigarette of the day. 'Tha's not a farmer then?'

'No, I'm a solicitor.'

'Ah reckoned tha'd be summat o' t' soart. Ah've nivver needed a solicitor yet, an' Ah 'ope Ah nivver do, if tha don't mind me sayin' so. Ah reckon me cricketin' days are ovver now - Ah'm eighty-five year old now, tha knows.'

Eighty-five, I thought to myself, as I tried to accept this statement. I reflected again that you never really come to terms with the people of your childhood getting older. It is for that reason I always think of my own mother as a perennial thirty-six year old playing endless games of rounders on Filey beach.

'Capstan' looked a lot older. His hair was pure white, his face was wrinkled and creased, his frame was bent and his movements were slow. Underneath, however, he still seemed the same person I had known all those years before; I saw him in my mind's eye, still cricketing, ferreting for rabbits, haymaking or struggling to start his old tractor, whilst puffing away at another cigarette underneath cloth cap and muffler.

'You look just the same to me - you haven't changed much at all', I said. 'We had some great times at your place when I was at school. I'll never forget your ice-cream.'

'T' pleasure were all mine, Ah reckons. It were grand tae 'ave sum childer round t' farm. It were a great sadness that t' missus and me nivver 'ad none of us own.'

He smiled as he remembered some of the pranks we got up to on his farm, and his cheerful face showed that he had lost none of his sense of humour.

A week or so later I happened to meet my old friend Doctor Meredith, the GP in Denley for many years, and I told him that I had seen 'Capstan' again, for I knew that he and his wife had been patients of his for many years.

'Do you know, John, I tried for nearly forty years to get him to give up smoking but when I saw him on his eighty-fifth birthday I actually advised him not to give it up, as the shock might kill him.'

I laughed out loud as I nodded my head in agreement, thinking he had done pretty well on cigs and ice-cream.

'The last time I saw him', Doctor Meredith continued, 'I had actually been to see Gladys, who now suffers very badly from rheumatism. I could hardly believe my eyes, John, when I got to their place. There was Gladys balanced precariously on a kitchen chair reaching up to put her washing on the line, while "Capstan" was sitting in the yard in a deck chair, a glass of whisky in his hand and clouds of tobacco smoke around his head. When Gladys eventually and very slowly and painfully got down and went into the kitchen, I turned to 'Capstan' and said:

'Good heavens, Mr Carter, you really can't allow your wife to do that sort of thing at her age and in her condition. I'm trying to treat her for rheumatism, you know.'

'Nay, doctor', replied 'Capstan', 'Ah gets a reight kick out o' seein' t' lass get up on t' chair, like.'

Again I couldn't help myself laughing out loud as my friend recounted this story, for the picture it conjured up in my mind was too hilarious for words.

A few weeks later I felt guilty about my laughter when I learnt that Gladys had died. When I visited her husband some little time afterwards I found that 'Capstan' was a much changed and broken man. This was very sad but not altogether surprising for, as I reflected afterwards, he had been married to her for nearly sixty years and to lose a lifelong partner must be devastating for anyone.

It was several months before I saw 'Capstan' after that. It was a bitterly cold winter's day, and as I was visiting a near neighbour of his on business I thought I would call in and see how he was getting on. I found 'Capstan' sitting in his favourite armchair huddled almost over the fire, obviously trying to keep warm. I was later to learn that a couple of days before my visit, an old farming friend of his had delivered a large tree trunk for 'Capstan' to reduce to logs. Sadly the old man had neither the money to pay for this to be done nor the strength to do it himself.

The sight which greeted me on entering his sitting room was one which would have been very funny if it had not been so tragic. Poor old 'Capstan' had succeeded in dragging the big, long trunk into his sitting room, and had somehow pulled the end of it over the fire. When the end bit was burnt, he pulled the trunk up a bit further. The tree trunk stretched from the fire to the back of the room. The effort involved in pulling it must have taken its toll, for my old friend looked totally exhausted as he slumped in the chair and held his hands out to feel the warmth of the fire.

I did my best to cheer him up and to make him comfortable, but he wasn't in the mood for talking and I left soon afterwards, feeling sad and depressed at his condition. The next week I arranged for a friend of mine to call with a saw to deal with the tree trunk and with a fresh supply of logs, but he found 'Capstan' collapsed on the living room floor and immediately arranged for him to be admitted to hospital.

When I heard what had happened I feared the worst could not be too long delayed. So when I visited my old friend in hospital no more than a week after his dramatic collapse, I expected to find him at death's door. As I entered his ward I could scarcely believe my eyes. There was old 'Capstan' sitting up in bed, looking as bright as a button and winking broadly in my direction as he chatted animatedly to a pretty young nurse.

'Na then, lad', he exclaimed in his old familiar way of greeting me. 'Tha's lookin' fair capped - Ah'm worth a good few dead 'uns yet, Ah reckons.'

I laughed out loud in relief and amusement.

'It's great to see you back to your old form, "Capstan". You'll soon be playing cricket again at this rate.'

'Aye, well mebbe me cricketin' days is ovver, but Ah'm goin' back tae Stocks Farm, tha knows.'

A gleam came into the old countryman's eyes just at the mention of his old farm, as he went on to tell me exactly how this remarkable turn of events had come about.

It transpired that it was all thanks to 'Capstan's' nephew Tom, who with his wife Linda had called to see him just three days before my own visit.

Now 'Capstan', possibly because he had no children of his own, had always been very fond of his nephew and had taken a great interest in his career. As a lad Tom had spent a lot of time at Stocks Farm and 'Capstan' always secretly hoped that one day he might perhaps take it over. Tom's father, however, had other ideas. He didn't see much future in farming, his son was academically bright and he persuaded him very much against his inclinations to go to university and make a career in accountancy.

Tom never settled in the profession his father had chosen for him. He felt confined and frustrated by office life and his longing for the open air and farming never left him. Just when he was despairing that his ambition would never be realised, he had that one great piece of luck which was to change his life completely.

His father-in-law, who had been a widower for some years, died suddenly of a heart attack. His very substantial fortune, which he had accumulated by thrift and a succession of inspired and lucrative speculations in property, stocks and shares, was inherited by his only daughter, Linda.

'Right Tom', said Linda to her husband soon after her father's funeral. 'Why don't we buy a farm? We can afford one now and it's what you've always wanted, isn't it?'

'Well, if you're sure', replied Tom hesitantly. 'It's your money after all. Anyway I'd have to go to agricultural college first. All I know about farming is what I picked up as a lad on my uncle's place at Stocks Farm.'

'Fine', replied his wife, 'but don't just talk about it, do it.'

So it was that Tom went to college as a mature student, and when he had finished his training he was ready to buy a farm and put his theoretical knowledge into practice.

Tom and Linda scanned the property section of the *Yorkshire Post* and as they did so there was one particular advertisement which caught Tom's eye.

'Well, I'll be blowed - do you see this, Linda?', he asked excitedly. 'Stocks Farm is on the market again. Do you think I was always meant to have it? This must be fate.'

Tom and Linda lost no time in making an offer for 'Capstan's' old farm, which was fairly soon accepted. The purchase had only just been completed when Tom heard about his uncle's condition and rushed to hospital to see him.

As he and Linda were making their journey to the hospital in the car, Tom suddenly had an idea, and his wife was soon in enthusiastic agreement.

'That's a brilliant idea, darling', she said. 'I just hope we're not too late.'

They nearly were, for when they finally arrived at the hospital they found 'Capstan' in a very poor state - frail, listless and looking to all the world as though he had lost the will to live.

He perked up the minute Tom told him about his purchase of Stocks Farm, and what his nephew had to say next not only surprised and delighted him - but as he later admitted to me, it quite literally saved his life.

'I may be book-wise, Uncle, and I know all about the business and accountancy side, but I've no practical experience of farming. Linda and I would like you to come and live with us at Stocks Farm and teach us all you know.'

As I stood at the side of the old man's hospital bed and heard him tell me all about his nephew's visit three days earlier, I realised just why it was that I had found my old friend so much better.

'Theer Ah were at death's door, lad, but like Ah were sayin', Ah'm worth a good few dead uns now, Ah reckon.'

'Capstan' was right. He now had a reason for living. Better still, Linda was a trained nurse, and was well qualified to care for him. To cap it all, she and Tom had two lovely boys, and of course 'Capstan' had always loved children.

The next time I saw 'Capstan' some weeks later he was happily installed back at Stocks Farm. Just being there seemed to bring strength back to his old limbs. I found him at the back of the mistal, surrounded by a horde of children who were queuing up for dollops of his home made ice-cream. He was clearly in his element again.

I think most of us would prefer to be remembered for what we were in our prime, and whenever I think of 'Capstan' I remember not the old man huddled over the fire trying to keep warm by a smouldering tree trunk, but of him dishing out dollops of ice-cream, playing cricket with myself and my friends, teaching us how to catch rabbits, how to drive his cranky old tractor, and sounding off his political opinions in a cloud of cigarette smoke at the Denley Heifer.

How splendid, I thought, as I left this happy scene at Stocks Farm, that another generation of children would hear old 'Capstan' say 'It's a poor belly that can't warm an ice-cream', and remember this remarkable countryman as I did.

Ashes to Ashes

There are many tasks which a solicitor has to perform as an executor or administrator of the estate of a deceased client: some are routine, others more difficult and a few very tricky indeed. There is the will to be looked out and its contents made known to the beneficiaries, there are forms to be completed, accounts to be prepared, papers to be sorted out and eventually money to be distributed, but before any of these steps can be taken there is the funeral.

Now if I were to attend every funeral, I would not have enough time for my work, so I have to be selective. Even then it can eat well into a working day. Only last week I went to the funeral of a Dales farmer - a church service, followed by a burial in another churchyard some miles up the dale, and rounded off by a splendid afternoon tea back at the farmhouse. Including travelling time, I was away from the office for nearly four hours!

Attending funerals may be optional, but if in my capacity as an executor I am required in the will to carry out certain duties, then perform them I must. Generally this requires no more than to administer the estate according to law and to invest money for infant beneficiaries, but now and again the duties go beyond the routine.

Sometimes a particular request will be made regarding burial or cremation; or occasionally asking for the body or part of it to be used for medical research. In such cases, the medical authorities will arrange for the ultimate disposal of the corpse, but they first have to decide whether or not it is suitable for use!

There are country people who still like to be buried, but most people these days prefer cremation, believing it to be quicker and cleaner. Ashes to ashes - and that's that.

On a few occasions over the years I have been charged in a will with the duty of scattering the ashes at some designated place - usually in some well-loved spot in the Dales countryside.

This is by no means as simple a job as would at first sight appear, particularly when you are challenged by the elements. You can be sure that on the day you have chosen to carry out this rather macabre duty, it will be a pouring wet day or, worse still, it will be blowing a gale - in which case, you have to position yourself correctly and be very careful indeed if you don't want to end up with the ashes all over your face!

In some well-known beauty spots the task has to be performed rather surreptitiously, because you know very well that if you apply for permission through official channels, there is almost certainly going to be a fee involved. It is also a job where you do not want any interruptions. It always takes longer than you think - sometimes the urn never seems to empty!

On one occasion I was right in the middle of scattering 'Uncle Joe's' ashes on a remote part of Denley Moor, where he had during his lifetime walked many a mile with his dog, when all of a sudden there was a voice behind me.

'What on earth are you doing, John?'

I turned around to see two of my oldest friends, Peter and Rachel Simpson, striding towards me with their dog Rover, having chosen this of all moments to walk on this particular stretch of isolated moorland.

'I'm scattering "Uncle Joe's" ashes. I'd stand well clear if I were you', I replied.

The expressions on Peter and Rachels's faces were a mixture of surprise, anxiety and horror as they rapidly backed away, but in their

56

confusion they completely failed to control their dog. Consequently Rover was jumping up at me, trying to knock the urn out of my hands, sniffing the ground where the ashes lay and generally making a thorough nuisance of himself as I tried to dispatch 'Uncle Joe's' last mortal remains with some degree of dignity.

My problems with Rover, however, were as naught compared with what happened when I came to distribute the ashes of Jack Higgins one day last summer.

Readers of my last book *Dales Law* may remember Jack Higgins, a real Yorkshire character but whose frequent appearances at my office always made me groan.

He was a man who knew his own mind, was used to getting his own way and was known up the dale as 'an ockard old bugger'. I well remember the time he stamped out of court muttering expletives about the damages he received for a slight neck injury in a road accident.

'Ah reckon that judge 'as nivver 'ad 'is neck in a bloody collar. It's disgustin' what 'e's givven us.'

I remember, too, his reaction when I told him that his claim to have 'summat knocked off t' price' for a table which turned out to be a tenth of an inch shorter then specified, would not succeed because the law did not concern itself with what it terms 'trivialities'.

'Trivialities, trivialities!' thundered Jack. 'Well, Ah can see Ah'm wastin' my time 'ere agin', he added, as he stood up and banged a large and horny fist down on my desk.

The very last time I had seen him alive was when he called at my office to ask if he could claim interest on a £50 loan to his own nephew who had been a month late in repaying.

Only a solicitor knows how incredibly mean, unreasonable and plain awkward some people can be.

Typically, Jack had been too tight to pay me to draw up a proper will. When he died, his nephew Jim (the one who should have paid the interest on his uncle's £50 loan) found a home-made will in which he and I were appointed executors. Jim Higgins, a pleasant, middle-aged man who does jobbing work on farms, came into my office looking slightly ill-at-ease as he handed over his uncle's home-made will.

'It looks like we've bin givven t' job tae do, like', said Jim quietly, pointing to the second clause of the will.

'I see what you mean', I replied, as I read that Jim and I were to scatter his ashes in Whetstone Beck just below the old packhorse bridge at Bents Ghyll.

'Ah knows 'e were an ockard old bugger - they all said t' same up t' dale - but we mustn't speak ill o' t' dead must we, Mr Francis?'

Jack's home-made will turned out to be a legal nightmare, but it was the scattering of his ashes at Whetstone Beck which I will never forget. It was a glorious summer day when Jim and I set off for Bents Ghyll with 't' ockard old bugger's' ashes in a splendid-looking old urn which I had wedged in the boot. The beauty and tranquility of the Dales that day contrasted oddly in my mind with the turbulence and discord represented by that most difficult client of mine who was now reduced to ashes.

Eventually we arrived at the packhorse bridge. Why Jack had chosen this particular place neither of us knew, but presumably it must have had some significance in his life - perhaps a place of happy childhood memories, who knows? At all events I started to empty the contents of the urn into the water, Jim electing to be a spectator rather than a participant in this somewhat distasteful event.

Unfortunately, from my point of view, there had been a prolonged drought, so that the stream had been reduced from its normal strong flow to a rather shallow trickle.

In trying to make sure that the ashes were thrown out into the middle of the current I obviously tried a bit too hard, and the reverse of what I intended actually occurred. Jack's ashes came out of the urn in one big wodge, just reached the edge of the current and then, to our embarrassment and dismay, eddied gently to the side of the stream and became stuck among some weeds.

'Typical', said Jim, 'just typical. 'E always were an ockard old bugger, an' be t' look o' things, death 'asn't changed owt.'

'What do we do now?', I asked myself out loud.

Before Jim had time to answer my question, I tried to answer it myself by giving the wodge of ashes a sharp push with the end of my walking stick.

This inspired manoeuvre had no effect at all, save to leave two wodges of ashes stuck instead of one and liberally coating the end of my walking stick with Jack's last mortal remains.

'Now that wasn't a very good idea', I said ruefully, as I tried to wipe my stick clean.

'Just leave 'im be', said Jim with a tone of exasperation in his voice. 'There nivver were no reasonin' wi' t' old bugger when 'e stuck fast in 'is opinion.'

As we walked back to the car, I was aware of Jim muttering again and again to himself as he shook his head:

'Just leave 'im be.'

My difficulties with the ashes of Uncle Joe and Jack Higgins were very real at the time, although rather humorous in recollection, but the strange experience I had when attempting to scatter the ashes of another long-standing acquaintance, Wilfred Farnham, falls into an altogether different category, for it was really one to make the hair stand on end. Even to write of it brings out an uneasy feeling, as if confirming what I have always believed, that there are more things in heaven and on earth than we mere humans will ever fully understand.

Wilfred Farnham had two main interests in life outside his family: the first was his wool business in Bradford, which he ran like a Victorian dictator, a benevolent one but a dictator all the same; the second - an unlikely one for a townsman - was beagling.

Wilfred's business life revolved around the famous but now defunct wool exchange near the town hall - a fine building, with a tower and a slender spire one hundred and fifty feet high, an open parapet and a statue of Saint Blaise, the patron of woolcombers. It was in the great hall, underneath a statue of Richard Cobden, where Wilfred used to meet his fellow merchants to buy and sell wool for the world.

In Wilfred's heyday, Bradford was the world's main market for wool textiles, the centre for the sorting of fleeces produced in England and brought from abroad, and for the process of combing which separates the long fibres from the short - the long fibres used for worsted cloth, the short for woollen cloth.

Wilfred lived in a large house on the outskirts of Bradford, but he didn't spend much time there, for he worked all hours. The wool trade has always been one of those industries where fortunes are there to be made, and where millionaires can lose all their money very quickly. Wilfred made his pile during the Korean War - a golden time for wool men, but he had been more far-sighted than most of his contemporaries. He had invested his money shrewdly in property, stocks and shares, and had over the years gradually wound down his business as trade became progressively harder during the sixties and seventies.

Wilfred's word was law, and he did not like his decisions to be questioned either in business or at home. His long-suffering wife

Freda once told me: 'Wilfred's always right about everything of course'.

He ruled his family the same way that he ran his business. He had to have the last word on everything, whether it was choice of carpet, a new refrigerator or even new clothes for his wife. If he had decided on the Isle of Wight for a holiday, then there his family would go; and if Lincoln Cathedral was beautiful and worth a visit, then it was beautiful and worth a visit. There was no reasoning or arguing with him - he knew at all times and on all occasions what was best for himself, his family and his workers.

In business Wilfred was tough to the point of being obstinate, though he was always fair and never did anything dishonest or deceitful. Everyone knew where they stood with Wilfred.

His wife Freda hated it on the odd occasion he deigned to go shopping with her, because he always bargained with shopkeepers and stallholders in a manner which would have graced an Arab bazaar.

'Na then, lad, what's t' best tha can do for us then?', was his usual opening shot even before he had examined the goods.

Yet underneath the bluff Yorkshire exterior was a man who genuinely cared for his family and his workers, though he rarely allowed these feelings to show.

Our first meeting was by arrangement at the wool exchange - or 'on change' as he called it - and I watched with interest as business was conducted in the time-honoured manner before he took me off to lunch at his club.

It was perhaps rather strange that Wilfred should have chosen a country solicitor like me to handle his legal work, but he was always anxious lest his fellow wool merchants should find out anything of his private business, and so he thought it safer to keep it 'out of town'. He had chosen me for no better reason than that a distant relative of his had been talking to him 'on change' about solicitors and had happened to mention that 'he knew a young feller up t' dale at Denley who wasn't a bad sort o' chap'.

Not that I ever had to do a great deal of work for him, for he never moved house and rarely became involved in litigation (a shake of the hand 'on change' was a man's bond in those days); but when he did it was a case of 'in litigation as in life', for like many others he was always convinced of the total infallibility and righteousness of his case. There was no arguing or reasoning with him, and the fact that I won the few cases he pursued only encouraged him.

I did manage to persuade him to make a will not long before he died. In it, he gave very precise instructions as to where his ashes were to be scattered. These stemmed from Wilfred's other great interest.

Wilfred was first introduced to the other passion of his life completely by chance. One Saturday in the early 1950s he had decided to take Freda for a run up the Dales, and had stopped to slake his thirst at a village pub. It so happened that the pub in question was the one chosen that day for the meet of the local beagles pack. As he walked into the pub with his wife, he found himself in the midst of a large number of jolly, weather-beaten country types, some of whom were wearing green hunting jackets and white trousers. There was a lot of drinking going on, as well as story-telling, and laughter. It is, as he learnt later, not for nothing that in rural communities such people are known as 'the merry beaglers'.

Wilfred found in the pub that day a close-knit, happy community, which in some ways was similar to the freemasonry of the wool merchants he met 'on change'.

He quickly got talking to some of 'the merry beaglers' and arranged to go out with them at the next meet. From that moment until the day he died, Wilfred was a committed member of the hunt. Just as some men are 'hooked' when they go fishing for the first time, or find that they have a natural golf swing or have an inbuilt feel for the rhythm of ballroom dancing, so Wilfred turned out to be one of those men who are born with a sporting instinct. It is an instinct which has nothing to do with class, social background, heredity or an ability to be good at games, but is born of a love of countryside, fresh air and exercise, and the music of hounds - that joyous chorus which dispels all cares and worries.

Wilfred took immediately to beagling like a duck to water. Soon he was learning the finer points and different aspects of the sport from various members of the hunting fraternity.

From old Professor Mackenzie, who at the age of eighy-five still followed hounds regularly, he learnt that hare-hunting has its roots deep in the past, that 'beagle' is a Celtic word meaning small, that the Roman poet Oppian had written of beagles in Britain, that the sport of hare-hunting dates to Saxon times and that it was the favourite pastime of Queen Elizabeth I.

From kennel huntsman Fred Black, Wilfred learnt all about hounds: how a pack of beagles should be steady, dogged and level, and how they needed good noses to follow a 'catchy' scent, a determined temperament and an ability to run forever. He was amazed to find that Fred knew all his hounds individually by name and he watched with awe as he saw the huntsman training them to 'hark to horn'.

From naturalist Barney Phipps he learnt all about hares - how they spend their lives hiding and running from danger, solitary, isolated and above ground. Barney told him that a good season for partridges was a good season for hares, and that where rabbits were plentiful, hares were not to be found. He soon understood too, as he watched the hunting, the true meaning of the expression 'to think like a hare', shown by their powers of concealment, speed, agility, and method of running.

From old Rex Halifax, the master of the hunt, he learnt how the hunt was run, how the field was kept in order and how the whippers-in helped to keep the pack together. He chuckled to himself one day when the master shouted to a young couple who were more interested in each other than what the hounds were doing:

'Did you hear me? I said hold hard, not hold hands.'

Being a Yorkshireman, Wilfred was delighted that his new-found hobby involved no equipment or expense. He discovered that he could take as much exercise on a day's beagling as he chose - he could run, walk or see what could be seen from his car. There was no need to overdo things. Someone told him that insanity was one of the chief requirements for the sport, and Wilfred soon showed the truth of this statement on days when he trudged around bleak Yorkshire moors in pouring rain. But whatever the weather Wilfred enjoyed himself, for he found that the worries of the week vanished, his lungs and arteries were cleared, and the cares of his sedentary life were washed away. Neither did he have any responsibilities - the only one was to turn up.

But perhaps best of all, Wilfred enjoyed the social side and the drinks in the pub after beagling, when he slaked his thirst, his tongue became loosened and he joined in the singing.

Wilfrd followed the beagles week in and week out, come rain or shine, for over forty years, and the last time he was out I stood with him by Buttersyke Wood - one of his favourite places, on the edge of Denley Moor. We watched together as the hounds raced off after a hare put up from her form, saw them cast round at a check and then work out by scent alone the intricate line the hare had taken.

The next time I was at Buttersyke Wood was to scatter his ashes there in accordance with his will, for very soon after his last day's beagling he died of a heart attack.

As I set off in my car with Wilfred's brother Philip, it seemed strange to think that Wilfred was no more, that he was gone, gone with the woollen mills and gone away with the merry beaglers of yesteryear who had given him so much pleasure.

The weather was good in Denley, but as all Dalesmen know, it is a different world up on the moors, and as we got out of the car, it was a good few degrees colder and there was a sharp, cutting wind. We shivered slightly as we walked over to Buttersyke Wood, that small copse of ancient deciduous trees adjoining the heather moorland where only a few weeks earlier I had stood with him and listened to the music of his favourite hounds.

As I stood silently for a minute I reflected that hares have always been the subject of folklore and were at one time associated with witchcraft and evil spells. The story has often been told in hunting circles of the time a hare ran into a farmyard and escaped from the pursuing hounds by getting inside a barn through a small opening. When the huntsmen eventually got the door open there was no sign of the hare inside, but there was an old hag sitting on a bale of straw. Curious, I thought, that there is lots of hare lore but so little exact hare knowledge.

As Philip and I prepared to spread Wilfred's ashes around his favourite spot, there was a terrible scream not too far distant which made us both jump.

'What on earth was that?', asked Philip.

'That, my friend', I replied, 'was the sound of a dying hare.'

Now I have never really believed the many legends there are of dedicated hunting men taking the form of their favourite quarry in the afterlife, but as I recovered from hearing the last cry of a dying hare and started to sprinkle Wilfred's ashes on the heather moorland around me, Philip suddenly shouted: 'Look!'

What I saw as I turned round may or may not have been a coincidence, but it sent a shiver down my spine and left a taste of fear in my mouth for the rest of the day.

A large brown hare came seemingly from nowhere and made fast progress up the heather moorland till I lost it from view on the skyline.

The Other Woman

Divorce nowadays is very much easier to obtain than it was in my early years as a solicitor. The main arguments about money, property and children still remain - and I suspect always will - but the actual process of getting a divorce is now quite simple, and in the case of undefended divorces does not even involve going to court. Petitions are filed, affidavits are sworn, an application for a divorce is made and a judge rubber-stamps it. A relationship sometimes of many years is brought to an end without fuss, ceremony or ritual. A decree is pronounced and that is that.

It is all a far cry from the tight rules of procedure and strict requirements of proof which were the stuff of nightmares for young solicitors a quarter of a century ago. At that time, you could only get a divorce in most cases if you could prove cruelty, desertion or adultery. If you had yourself committed adultery, it was a bar to divorce unless you could persuade the judge to 'exercise discretion' in respect of it. This in turn often depended on the temper and prejudices of the judge in question; some judges were more easily persuaded than others.

Cruelty cases took the longest, depending on how many instances of beatings, hittings and violence the judge wanted to hear about. It has never ceased to amaze me how many women are prepared to suffer violence at the hands of their husbands for so long. In theory, desertion was the easiest to prove, had it not been for the absurd rules of evidence which required the person asking for a divorce to remember dates and incidents rather than be 'led' by their solicitor or barrister. This always struck me as ludicrous, bearing in mind that the person asking for a divorce had already signed a divorce petition setting out the relevant allegation, and all that should have really been necessary was one question asking for those allegations to be confirmed.

In one desertion case, my client was a desperately anxious lady who was highly nervous at the prospect of giving evidence in open court. I tried to reassure her beforehand by telling her that the only date she had to remember was the one when he left home for good.

'Did there come a time when you and your husband separated?', I asked.

'Yes', she replied almost inaudibly.

'What happened?'

'He left me', she whispered, dissolving into tears.

'When did that happen?'

There was a pause, but no reply.

I repeated the question.

There was still no reply.

Even though I had gone over the case with her carefully, and she had repeated the date to herself a number of times before we came into court, she had obviously gone completely blank under the strain and no amount of cajoling on my part was going to unfreeze her mind.

In the end I was faced with two choices: either I had to ask the judge to adjourn the case, which would have caused the woman great distress; or I could fly in the face of the rules of evidence and 'lead' her. I decided on the latter, and incurred the wrath of the judge in doing so.

'You should know better than that, Mr Francis', he scolded, looking sternly at me over his spectacles.

I stoically accepted the rebuke, for the poor woman got her divorce decree and I was satisfied.

Cruelty and desertion cases had their difficulties but adultery cases formed a category of their own. The main figures in such cases were private investigators or enquiry agents. Their evidence was sometimes sad, other times dramatic - and occasionally hilarious.

The stereotype of the private detective portrayed in the media is a rather seedy, life-battered character living in a twilight world of bedsits and always wearing a mackintosh. In truth the detectives I used to employ were not at all like that; they were usually rather respectable ex-police officers who were well-regarded by the divorce judges. Their frequent and regular appearances tended to forge and cement a rather cosy relationship of 'mutual admiration'. This was a distinct advantage for, when I was floundering or the evidence was not coming up to scratch, the day would often be saved by the testimony of the private detective.

The easiest way for a detective to obtain proof of adultery was to take statements from the erring spouse and his or her partner confessing it and their signatures would then be identified by the person asking for a divorce.

The more challenging cases were those where adultery was denied, and observation had to be carried out in the hope that suspicion could be turned into proof. It was difficult, not to say embarrassing, to catch a couple actually *in flagrante*, so what was required was proof of intention and opportunity.

Sometimes, of course, people were aware that they were being followed and spied on. In one case my client told me that her husband always met his girlfriend in a certain pub and then left to spend a night together at an unknown destination. So I arranged for Bill Hammond, one of the most experienced detectives in the area, and a good friend and colleague, to observe them in order to obtain evidence of adultery. Bill made contact in the pub, and then spent three hours watching them whilst making a pint of Tetleys last a very long time. He left when they did, and he followed at what he thought was a discreet distance as they left the pub car park.

Bill had only followed them a hundred yards down the road when they suddenly stopped. He also stopped and observed the driver's window being wound down. A hand emerged, and that well-known V-sign was given by the driver.

'I knew it was time for me to go home then!', he told me later.

On other occasions, Bill was more successful. He once observed a couple in a car from a distance, and his description of the violent rocking of the car was sufficient to infer sexual intercourse. On another occasion he booked into a hotel bedroom adjoining that of the suspected couple, and with his ear pinned to a fortunately thin dividing wall was able to discern certain unmistakable sounds and movements, which were again enough to satisfy the court of adultery.

Normally such investigations yield speedy results, either in the form of 'confession statements' or of compromising situations from which the court could infer adultery.

Very occasionally, suspicion proved to be unfounded or no evidence could be obtained. Husbands' and wives' explanations for being away from home can actually be true. Husbands do sometimes genuinely work late at the office, and wives sometimes really do stay for weekends with old schoolfriends.

Monica Jones wore a sad and sorry expression the day she called at my office to discuss her matrimonial affairs. She was then aged about forty-five, but still had a good figure, and if she had not been so upset and tearful she would have looked a very attractive woman indeed. She was well dressed, with the unusual combination of brown hair and grey-green eyes. It was hard on the face of it to believe that her husband would have wanted to look elsewhere.

'I don't know where to begin, Mr Francis', she said.

This is an opening comment I have heard so often, and I have over the years developed a standard reply to it.

'Just begin wherever you like.'

I usually like to talk first in a matrimonial case. It seems impersonal somehow to start taking down details of marriage, occupation, residence and dates of birth of children. The details can be put to paper later. The important thing is to put the person at ease and let him or her talk. It can take some time to establish the necessary confidence; members of the general public sometimes feel nervous meeting

69

a solicitor for the first time, and will often more readily describe the intimate problems of their married life to the office receptionist.

Monica started to shed a few tears, which rapidly turned into a flood.

'Don't worry', I said. 'Try not to upset yourself.'

This attempt to comfort her only produced more tears.

'I'll get you a cup of coffee', I said.

Coffee in my experience is a godsend in such situations, and after she had drained the cup the tears suddenly dried up.

'I'm sorry, Mr Francis, but I'm still recovering from the shock. I just can't believe it.'

'What can't you believe, Mrs Jones?', I asked gently.

'That Richard's seeing another woman. If you knew him, Mr Francis, you'd know that he's just not the type.'

I made no comment on this particular observation. It is one which I have heard many times before, and I know very well from my experience as a man and a lawyer that there is no particular type of the male species who is immune to this particular temptation. I asked her a question instead.

'How do you know he's seeing another woman?'

'Well, he usually comes home for lunch every Wednesday, but last Wednesday he said he couldn't because he had a business lunch in town.'

'Well, perhaps he was having a business lunch in town', I said, not wishing to rule out the possibility of an innocent explanation.

'He was having lunch alright, but it wasn't with a business colleague. A friend of mine, Penny Simpson, said she'd seen him with a young woman over in Grassdale just coming out of a pub.'

'Well, there still might be an innocent explanation', I said without too much confidence.

'There might be, Mr Francis, except that he lied to me about it. I asked him that night if he had had a successful business lunch in Denley, and he said that it had been a particularly good meeting with all sorts of important decisions being taken. It's the fact that he lied and not so much what that old gossip Penny said which has

71

convinced me he's having an affair. I still can't believe it but it must be true.'

'Have you said anything to him?' I asked.

'No, not yet. I want to know all the facts first and that's why I've come to you. Can you recommend a good detective?'

'If it's true, Mrs Jones, do you want to divorce him?'

'Well, I can't compete with an attractive younger woman. He must have been suddenly hit by a mid-life crisis - perhaps he felt that life was passing him by or something. But I still can't believe it, we've been so happy together.'

'I can recommend a good private detective if you're sure that's how you want to proceed, but do think about it first. Do you really want to know the details of this relationship? It might just be a flash in the pan - sometimes it can be better not to know.'

'I've made my mind up, Mr Francis. I want to know what's going on. Will you please instruct a detective for me.'

'Yes, if that's what you want, but I shall need a recent photo of your husband as well as a some details of where he works, his car and so on.'

I duly took down the details, and when she had given me a photo, I asked Bill Hammond to carry out observations and report back.

I heard nothing from him for three weeks, so I thought I had better give him a ring because Monica kept enquiring as to progress.

'Can I come round and talk, John?'

'Yes, if you like, but can't you just send me a report?'

'This is one of the strangest case I've come across and I can't get to the bottom of it.'

Bill came round to see me at the office later that day.

'Well?' I said expectantly.

'He's seeing a young woman alright. I've followed him closely this past three weeks and they've met about seven times, always in a pub or restaurant right out of Denley, but they've not spent the night together.'

'Have you followed her?'

'Yes, she always comes in her own car and one night I followed her back to a house in Leeds. I found out next day that she is a student at the university and shares the house with five other students. I don't know what to make of it, John. I can't remember a case quite like this before. Do you want me to follow them for another week?'

'Right, Bill, we'll just try one more week and see if anything develops.'

A week later Bill was back in my office.

'Have you made any progress?' I asked eagerly.

'None at all, John', he replied, 'It's exactly the same pattern as last week - pubs, restaurants and a chaste goodnight kiss. I can't reckon this job up at all.'

I was silent for a minute as I considered how we should now proceed with the investigation.

'What do we know about Richard - his background, that sort of thing?', I asked.

'I haven't been able to find out very much. He comes from quite a rich family. His father was in business in Bradford and Richard went to university in London, I was told. He was reading law - his father wanted him to be a solicitor but it seems Richard didn't, and he dropped out after his first year and joined his father's business.'

As I listened to Bill I realised that Richard must have been at London at about the same time that I was starting my first year at Leeds University. I remembered, too, that I had a schoolfriend called Peter Armistead who had gone to London University to read law. I decided to give Peter a ring to see if he could tell me anything more about Richard and his time at university.

'Right, Bill, I'll make a few enquiries of my own. You've done enough for the moment.'

It took me a few days to make contact with Peter. I had not been in touch with him for at least twenty years, but I eventually managed to track him down through mutual acquaintances and got hold of his telephone number.

To say that Peter was surprised to hear from me when I got through to him would be a considerable understatement.

'To what do I owe this pleasure?', he asked.

'It's lovely to speak to you again - we really must get together some time - but the real reason I'm phoning you is professional, so I'd be grateful if you would keep this conversation confidential.'

'Whatever have I done now?' asked Peter, who was obviously becoming rather worried at the turn the conversation was taking.

'It's not about you', I reassured him, 'it's about a chap who was at university with you, name of Richard Jones - do you remember him?'

'The name does ring a bell somewhere.'

'He left at the end of the first year - he decided he didn't want to do law.'

'Yes, John, now you've told me that, I remember him very well - but there was another reason why he left at the end of his first year.'

'Well, what was it?' I asked.

'If you don't mind, John, I don't think it's something I'd like to talk about on the telephone. Perhaps we should meet and have that pint together.'

'Just as you like, Peter. You're in Sheffield and I'm in Denley - where shall we meet?'

'It's years since I came to Denley. How about the Denley Heifer?'

'It's a long way for you to come.'

'That doesn't matter - I can bring my wife over and she can look round the shops while we have a chat.'

'Alright, then. See you next Saturday at half past twelve.'

It was with a sense of anticipation and curiosity that I went to meet Peter. I just couldn't think what there was about Richard's time at university which could call for such secrecy and discretion.

'Now, John', said Peter after we had finished our first pint and caught up on old times. 'You wanted to know about Richard Jones and why he left at the end of his first year at university?'

'I thought it was because his father had pushed him into reading law and he decided it wasn't for him.'

'Well, that may have been partly the reason but there was another one, you know. I didn't want to talk about it on the phone. There was a scandal involving Richard and we all felt rather guilty about it. He was a very quiet, studious and rather serious young man when he

74

started at university. We all decided to do something about it. When he'd been there about three months we took him out with us on a pub crawl, mixed his drinks pretty wickedly and got him absolutely plastered. The last pub we went to, there was a rather attractive barmaid who seemed to take a fancy to him even in the drunken state he was in, and she told us to clear off at closing time and said she would take him home. Well, he didn't come home that night and I think you can guess the rest, John. She became pregnant and had her baby. Richard's father paid her a generous capital sum on the understanding that neither she nor the child should ever contact him or any member of his family. I don't know whether any of this helps you, John, but I've told you all I can remember. I haven't seen Richard since he left university.'

'Just one more question, Peter - was the baby a boy or a girl?'

'I'm not absolutely sure', he replied, 'but I heard it was a girl.'

The next week I met Richard by arrangement at his office and told him why I had come to see him. The time had come, I felt, to bring matters to a head.

'It's your daughter you have been seeing isn't it, Mr Jones?'

'How do you know that?'

'Well, it doesn't really matter how I know, but it's true, isn't it?'

In a strange way Richard looked relieved, as if the burden of months of deceit had been lifted from his shoulders.

'Yes, it's true, Mr Francis. I've been happily married for years, but as time went by I seemed to have this yearning to see the daughter I had never known. It was a hell of a job to find her but I did, and I'm glad I did. It's been wonderful seeing her but I'm worried sick about Monica's reaction. My marriage means everything to me. What should I do now, Mr Francis?'

'You'll have to talk to Monica because I have to tell her the result of my enquiries.'

'What shall I tell her?'

'How about the truth?', I replied.

Later that day I telephoned Monica.

'Well, Mr Francis, have you found out what's going on?'

'Yes I have, Mrs Jones, but I don't want to say anything more on the phone. I've spoken to your husband earlier today and he will be talking to you tonight.'

'Can't you tell me anything?'

'I'll just say one thing, Mrs Jones. It isn't what you think. It isn't what you think at all.'

Taken In

Even a solicitor who is by reputation cautious, prudent and sensible is not immune to the wiles of a good conman. During my career I have on two occasions been completely taken in by conmen. They both seemed so genuine at the time, but then that is what all victims say and why these people are so successful in what they do.

The first such case happened many years ago. Perhaps I can forgive myself in retrospect for being taken in, because I was a fairly newly-qualified solicitor with only limited experience of legal practice in particular and life in general. I think most people, whatever their trade, profession or vocation, have much to learn and are somewhat naïve in their approach when they are let loose on the great British public for the first time. Most people are decent, friendly and thoroughly respectable, but there are always a few scoundrels, oddballs, cheats and rogues in every walk of life.

The gentleman who came into my office was someone I'd never seen before but, as I realised later, he never gave me the chance to ask him many questions as he talked nearly all the time himself. All I knew at this stage was his name - Jack Pearce.

'I'm just back in England after spending the last ten years in Canada. I've made a pile in the timber trade and I reckoned it was time to come back to the old country, buy a house, find a wife, raise a family and settle down.'

As he spoke he looked to me just like a man who might well have spent some time in Canada or indeed anywhere in the great outdoors. He was a tall, handsome man, well-built with a swarthy, weather-beaten face. I could just imagine him working with a gang of loggers in the Canadian timber trade. I had no reason whatever to suspect him or his story.

I was in truth rather fascinated by this character who had walked off the street into my office, and I was tempted to sit back and listen to the many tales I felt sure he had of his experiences in Canada. I had many jobs to do that day, however, and felt I must get on with the business in hand.

'What can I do for you, Mr Pearce?', I asked.

'Why, Mr Francis, I've already found a little place that's just what I'm looking for and I want you to handle the legal side of it for me. I hear good reports of you in Denley.'

I warmed to this compliment and quickly - perhaps too quickly - replied.

'Yes, of course, I'll be delighted to act for you if you can give me the details.'

He produced the sales particulars from a local estate agent, and I couldn't conceal a gasp of surprise as I saw the photograph of 'the little place' Mr Pearce said he had decided to buy. It looked a superb property in every way - a large detached house with five acres of land, a swimming pool, two bathrooms, landscaped gardens, and priced at over £100,000 - which in those days was a considerable sum of money.

'This is a very expensive property, Mr Pearce', I said. 'How are you going to pay for it?'

'No problem, Mr Francis, no problem, at all', he replied. 'I've got it in cash - it's all there waiting in Canada.'

I then asked him a few questions about how the money was to be transferred from Canada to this country, which he answered confidently and in a manner which suggested that he had thoroughly investigated and mastered all the laws, regulations and procedures relating to the exchange controls in force in those days.

'If you're paying cash for the house, I think it would be wise to have a private survey done', I advised.

'Sure', replied Mr Pearce, 'if you think that's what I need, then go right ahead and commission one.'

After he had left the office I telephoned local estate agent, surveyor and valuer Dick East and asked him to carry out the survey. Within a week his written report was on my desk and it contained no surprises. The property Mr Pearce wished to buy he described as 'undoubtedly one of the most outstanding houses in the area and arguably the best I have ever had the honour of surveying in over twenty years'.

Over the next few weeks I did not see Mr Pearce again, but I did receive a number of telephone calls asking about progress. I told him that I had obtained an excellent surveyor's report, the enquiries I had raised on the draft contract were all answered satisfactorily, and as soon as I had received the result of the local authority search I would be in a position to go through all the documents with him with a view to exchanging contracts and fixing a completion date. The transaction was proceeding smoothly - much too smoothly, as I was to reflect later.

The day that I received a clear local search, and was about to contact Mr Pearce for an appointment, I received a telephone call from Peter Davies, the partner in the firm of estate agents handling the sale of the property, who was also a good friend of mine.

'I'm sorry to trouble you, John, and I hope you don't mind me saying what I'm going to say - but do you think Mr Pearce is going to buy this house. How much do you actually know about him? I'm worried that he's only looked at the house once and he couldn't have spent more than ten minutes there. I'd have expected him to have gone back a time or two.'

For the first time doubts began to surface at the back of my mind.

'Well, actually Peter, I don't know him at all. It's the first time I've acted for him. He told me he'd been in Canada for the past ten years.'

'Yes - in the timber trade - he told me all about that, but has he really got the money to pay for this place?'

My doubts began to increase with every word.

'Well, he had all the right answers about exchange controls when I asked him', I replied.

'He gave me all the right answers too, but all of a sudden I've got a bad feeling about this. Somehow I just don't think he's going to sign the contract.

'Well, we'll soon find out', I replied. 'I've just got the local search back and I'm about to make an appointment with him. He's staying at the Denley Arms you know.'

'I may be wrong, John, but I just feel uneasy about this one. Cheerio, let me know what happens won't you?'

I put the telephone down and immediately picked it up again to call the Denley Arms. My anxiety increased when the receptionist told me that Mr Pearce was no longer there and would I please speak to the manager, Eric Garside.

'It looks as if we've both been had, Mr Francis. Our Mr Pearce did a moonlight last night. He owes me for the time he's been staying here, and what's worse he's borrowed a lot of money from some of my other guests. Told them he was a millionaire, made his pile in the timber trade in Canada and was just waiting for the money to be transferred to this country.'

My worst fears were suddenly realised as I listened to Mr Garside's story.

'Have you reported him to the police?', I asked.

'Of course I have, and a detective inspector came round within a few minutes. Told me this man was very well known to the police throughout the country. Sometimes he calls himself Jack Pearce who's made a fortune in the Canadian timber trade, other times he's Jock Peters who's just arrived back in the old country after making his pile in South African gold mines. He's played this trick from Lands End to John O' Groats according to the police. The funny thing is he seemed so genuine. We all fell for him hook, line and sinker. He said all the right things.'

80

'Yes', I repeated ruefully, 'he did say all the right things. That's what all good conmen do, I suppose. We're just not really prepared for them in Denley, are we?'

'What have you lost then, Mr Francis?'

'Oh, just my own fees, the cost of a survey fee and my own pride in not spotting him', I replied.

As things turned out I did not have to pay Dick East for the survey, for when I rang him to put him in the picture he was both generous and sympathetic.

'Well', he said, 'it could have been a damn sight worse. We might have had an exchange of contracts and a completion which didn't happen. You don't owe me anything for the survey. I enjoyed doing it. It was one of the best properties I've ever seen. Let's both put it down to experience, eh, John?'

'That's very decent of you, Dick', I said, 'but there's one thing I don't get in the case. I can understand our friend staying at fine hotels and "borrowing" money from people up and down the country. That's how he lives and that's his con, but why should he instruct solicitors and estate agents to buy a luxury house when the transaction could not possibly go through. What on earth does he get out of it?'

'I reckon it is all part of his act', replied Dick, 'I remember a middle-aged, perfectly respectable-looking man once coming into my office after viewing one of our best and most expensive properties for sale and saying simply "I'll have it". I never saw or heard from him again. It must just have given him some sort of kick. The same goes for our friend, I suppose.'

'I suppose that can be the only explanation', I replied.

But I was still kicking myself, a rather cautious Yorkshire solicitor after all, for not hearing warning bells at an earlier stage.

I don't think I'm likely, ever again, to believe anyone who comes into my office with a story about making a fortune abroad, and having some difficulty in arranging for the cash to be transferred. I suppose this is why so many Yorkshiremen like to see the colour of someone's money or 'brass' before doing business with them. I remembered particularly Jack's words to me on our first meeting: 'No problem, Mr

Francis, no problem at all'. Ever since I was conned by Jack Pearce I have always reacted with extreme caution and suspicion to anyone who says 'no problem'.

The second occasion on which I was completely taken in was rather unusual, and perhaps in retrospect I should not be too hard on myself for failing to spot it. I was working hard in my office as usual one day, when my secretary Clare interrupted to say that a young man was in reception and needed to see me immediately if I could possibly manage to fit him in. Now when people ask to see me in such polite terms I am far more likely to agree than when they belligerently demand immediate attention.

'Alright, Clare, tell him I can give him a quarter of an hour now. I can just put him in between drafting that lease I should have done two weeks ago and preparing instructions to counsel on the Duxbury case. What's his name by the way, and what's it about?'

'His name is Jason Portman and he wouldn't say what it's about.'

'Jason Portman', I repeated. 'I can't think of anyone in Denley by that name. He doesn't sound like a local.'

'Good morning, Mr Portman, I don't think we've met before', I said as I ushered him in and invited him to take a seat. 'I'm afraid I can't spare much time this morning, so what can I do for you?'

'It's perfectly alright', replied Mr Portman. 'I won't take up much of your valuable time, I promise you. Can you make a will for me. I'm afraid I shall have to ask you to do it as quickly as possible. I've been to see my doctor this morning and he told me to put my affairs in order. I've been given a maximum of two months to live.'

Now a solicitor can be told many things which cause him neither surprise nor embarrassment, but what Mr Portman had to say to me completely shook my equilibrium. Firstly I felt cross with myself for talking about my valuable time. Secondly I felt humble in the presence of someone who was facing the prospect of imminent death with so much fortitude, calmness and bravery.

I felt even worse when Jason went on to tell me that he had no family of his own and was trying to see all his friends around the country to say goodbye.

'Can't the doctors do anything for you?', I asked.

'I'm afraid not, Mr Francis. I've just come out of hospital. They've given me my last transfusion. You see, I've got a very rare blood disorder. There's only a handful of cases on record, but it's always terminal.'

I sat back again in wonder at the brave, matter-of-fact way Jason was apparently accepting his fate.

I took down the instructions for the will, which were very simple as Jason was leaving everything he had to certain named medical charities. I decided this was a case for handwriting the will and completing it there and then.

'I'm so sorry, Mr Francis', said Jason, feeling his pockets. 'I haven't brought my chequebook with me or I'd have paid you now',

'Don't worry about that', I said sympathetically. 'You've given me your London address for the will. Just tell me where you're staying in Denley and I'll send you a copy of the will along with my bill.'

'That's alright, Mr Francis, I'll pop in tomorrow before I leave for Scotland. I'll collect the copy and pay your bill then.'

'Fine', I replied. 'Whereabouts in Scotland are you staying?'

'Galloway - you know the Border country John Buchan wrote about in *The Thirty-Nine Steps*?'

'Oh, you're a Buchan fan too are you?'

There was no holding me then, and thoughts of the Duxbury file went completely out of my mind for the next hour or so as Jason and I talked - and talked and talked some more. As I eventually showed him to the door, I reflected that I might at least for a time have taken his mind off the dreadful prospect he was facing so bravely.

Jason did not appear at my office the next day, and I couldn't get him out of my mind: perhaps his brave, laughing manner had been just that, and deep down he was heading for a nervous breakdown. Who wouldn't?, I thought, facing such a crisis. I wondered about ringing the police, but quickly realised that I did not have a local address for him. Two days later there was a note which had been put in our post box with the rest of the mail. My anxiety increased as I read it.

'Dear Mr Francis,

It was kind of you to see me the other day. I'm very sorry that I didn't call in to collect the copy will and pay your bill. I'm sure you understand that I've a lot on my mind. In fact I've decided what I'm going to do. Chris at the Samaritans knows all about it. You'll probably read about it in the papers. So long. I enjoyed our chat.

Best Wishes

Jason.'

As I read the note I realised with increasing concern that Jason's brave appearance had indeed been an act. I feared the worst had probably already happened as I noted his references to 'a decision' and to the Samaritans. I immediately telephoned the local Samaritans and asked for Chris. There was a momentary silence at the other end of the line when I had completed my story of Jason Portman. The reply when it came was not what I expected.

'Jason Portman again', he said. 'Sometimes it's Jason Portman, other times James Parker or Jeremy Parfitt. What was he dying of this time - leukaemia, a bullet in the brain that couldn't be removed or a rare blood disorder?'

'I'm sorry, but I find this hard to believe', I said, trying to come to come to terms with this totally unexpected disclosure.

'You're not the first one, Mr Francis. He's known to hospitals and Samaritans throughout the country - we've all got him on file.'

'But I don't understand', I replied. 'What does he get out of it?'

'Strange thing is human psychology, Mr Francis. He must get something out of it.'

'When you think about it', I mused, 'he must need help of some sort.'

'I wouldn't worry about it too much, Mr Francis. You may have helped him more than you realise. Perhaps we both have.'

The White Blackbird

It is inevitable in a busy solicitor's practice that there are many people whose names and cases one forgets. There are some, however, who linger in the memory, either because they were rather special themselves or their cases were out of the ordinary, particularly difficult or just interesting.

I shall certainly never forget Donald and Margery Wigton, who lived all their long married life in the delightful lower Dales village of Fordingley. They became my clients soon after I qualified as a solicitor, and I was a guest at their golden wedding some twenty years later which they celebrated with a splendid reception at the village hall - a reception to which seemingly just about everyone in the village had been invited.

It struck me then - as it has done forcibly many times over the years - that every village has its Donald and Margery: a couple who have lived there all their lives, who know everyone and everything that is going on, who are part and parcel of just about every local organisation and whose names are automatically synonymous with the name of the village itself.

Donald and Margery had first met at university, where he was reading mathematics and she was a medical student. Donald was actually born in Lancashire, but when Margery invited him to her parent's home in Fordingley, he immediately fell in love with the village, its people and the surrounding countryside. He also fell in love with Margery, although she was not immediately aware of it. Indeed, their first evening alone together was not an unqualified success. Margery cooked a meal - a meal which she had gone to a deal of trouble to prepare. Afterwards, Donald leaned back in his chair in a self-satisfied manner before remarking:

'You're not a bad cook, Margery. In fact I might marry someone like you one day.'

Margery, who was undoubtedly a feminist before her time, was distinctly unamused.

It was from this rather unpromising start that their romance grew and blossomed. Margery, who was the only daughter of the village doctor, found in Donald the perfect partner. He was a brilliant mathematician; and Margery, who had followed her father into the medical profession, was clever, well-read and intellectually stimulating. He soon discovered that she was a lot more than a good cook. She found, too, that they had many more interests in common: religion, amateur dramatics, gardening and natural history, and above all a desire to serve.

This shared desire to serve was illustrated by the jobs they chose when they had graduated and decided to get married. Margery joined her father in his far-flung country medical practice, and Donald, who could undoubtedly have pursued a distinguished academic career in higher education, went to teach maths at the nearest grammar school.

They had arranged to rent a small cottage in Fordingley, but only weeks after their wedding day Margery's parents were tragically killed in a car crash. She and Donald moved into their house in which they were to live for the whole of their married life.

As they were to recall later, these early days were not easy. At a time when lady doctors were a rarity, Margery had to step into her father's shoes at a very young age, and try to persuade his highly conservative and sceptical patients that she was 'a proper doctor' and as equally well-qualified to look after them as her father. For Donald, too, it was not easy to accept that he had a working wife who was often on call at night and during weekends, the only times they could be together. They had some domestic help in the house, but it was an unusual marriage for those days.

Neither could be consoled when Margery had an accident out riding. The tragic result was that she would never be able to have children of her own.

After long and anxious discussions they decided against adoption, and reacted to their grief by throwing themselves even more energetically into serving their community. In truth they very soon became involved in just about everything that was going on in Fordingley.

They were both leading lights in the local amateur dramatic society; Donald was church treasurer and Margery a stalwart member of the choir. Both helped to run the youth club, and were involved one way or another in nearly all the sporting activities in the village. Donald played for the football team till he was forty-five, and regularly turned out for the cricket eleven, in which he gained a reputation as a steady bat and an accurate slow left arm bowler. They also played first couple for the tennis club, and unusually for a husband and wife combination, they did so remarkably happily.

Donald eventually retired from his position as senior maths master at the grammar school. He was undoubtedly the 'Mr Chips' of his day, having taught generations of schoolchildren, and guided and helped a succession of head teachers. He was of the old school of teachers - chalk and talk delivered from the front of the class in front of the blackboard and in an atmosphere of quiet attentiveness. He was a strict disciplinarian, but never needed to exert it much, as he was a born teacher with an ability to explain difficult concepts in a simple way and to make even a dry subject like mathematics interesting.

He had taught in the same classroom for nearly forty years, when he suddenly realised that a new generation of teachers was arriving with very different standards and attitudes. His time-honoured dress of old sports jacket with leather patches on the elbows and cavalry twills stood out from the jeans and open-necked shirts of some of the younger teachers. He, too, noticed that they were on first-name terms with the children, whom, to his ill-concealed disapproval, they always referred to as 'the kids'.

'A kid is a baby goat', he remarked to his wife, when complaining to her about this practice.

When Donald retired, so naturally did Margery, and by the time of their golden wedding they had both been retired for some ten years. They were at last able to have the time to enjoy those things they had enjoyed in their courting days fifty years earlier: walks in the country, meals together at favourite pubs, rediscovering old haunts and finding new special places. But their great shared delight was their garden, which Donald at the age of seventy-five still insisted on looking after without any help. The old house was really too big for them but neither could bear to leave it.

Donald's artistic talents emerged in the garden, where his mixed borders always displayed in high summer a glorious combination of colours. His talents outside were neatly complemented by Margery's gift with house plants, always neatly potted and colourful in the conservatory. In their retirement they loved to sit together in there, enjoying the garden, watching the birds, drinking coffee and doing the crossword together.

Well into their retirement Donald and Margery were still very much at the hub of village life. On any question arising as to what particular course should be taken or on any point of village history, the first thing anyone would ask was: 'Have you spoken to Donald or Margery?'

Although not quite always agreeing with one another in committee, they would never be disloyal to one another. They had both of course watched the village change over the years. In particular, there had in recent years been an influx of 'off comed-uns' whose views and attitudes often differed sharply from those of the original village people. The wise newcomers, they noticed, would play themselves in for a time without trying to impose their own views or bring about rapid changes. Donald and Margery knew better than anyone that country people can be led and influenced, but they will not be driven. They had both nearly resigned from the village hall committee some five years previously, when Donald had taken exception to just such an ill-considered remark by one of the 'off comed-uns'. Margery had immediately stood up and declared: 'If Donald goes, I go too', whereupon one of the older villagers called for a vote of confidence, which was immediately carried by a large majority.

'Don't you realise what Donald and Margery have done for the village - we couldn't manage without them'.

Talking about the meeting later that evening as they had a cup of tea together before bedtime, Donald said to his wife:

'Maybe it's time they did manage without us. Perhaps it's the right time for us to retire from some of these jobs - time for the younger ones to take over. We've had a good innings, and anyway we've both had a lifetime of committees and organising things. There's lots of other things in life, after all.'

They had always done everything together. Retirement seemed only to cement their relationship, as they walked, talked and gardened together. They were absolutely inseparable. They continued to learn from each other. Donald had an encyclopaedic knowledge of both wild and garden flowers, and Margery continued to astound her husband with her unerring ability to identify literally every type of British bird and, amazingly to him, an ability to recognise birdsong even when it was so distant that he had not even heard it. They enjoyed testing each other on their specialised fields of knowledge.

'Which flowers', asked Margery, 'did Shakespeare describe as "painting the meadows with delight"?'

'Why, lady's smock, of course', replied Donald. 'That's an easy one. Do you remember those halcyon days when we were students and went on that trip to Stratford-upon-Avon to see *Othello* and walked among meadows white with lady's smock. Talking of halcyon days, what exactly is a halcyon?'

'That's an easy one too', replied Margery. 'A halcyon is a kingfisher, a bird whose hatching season was fabled to be always accompanied by calm weather. The halcyon days are literally the seven days preceding and the seven days succeeding the winter solstice while the kingfisher is breeding.'

They became acutely aware in their retirement that the seasons of the dale, like life itself, are come and gone all too quickly, that the spring freshness of youth had developed into the maturity of middle age and on into the golden days of an Indian summer. There came, too, the realisation that the flowers they loved so much would wither and die, the birds would cease to sing and that the splendours of the changing seasons and the wonders of life itself must be grasped and enjoyed while they were still able to do so.

Margery hardly needed to travel beyond her beloved garden, for all the birds of the district seemed to know that it was a paradise and a sanctuary presided over by one who knew them, loved them and seemed to have an intuitive, almost spiritual, empathy with them.

Her bird table was always alive with robins, tits, finches, sparrows and nuthatches; but her particular delight were the swallows, which unfailingly returned every year to build their nests under the thatched roof of the old summerhouse.

Donald and Margery were well into their eighties before I noticed any change in them. I visited them one glorious June day to discuss their wills, and for the first time I thought Donald looked an old man and Margery seemed quite frail and walked with difficulty.

As her husband made tea, Margery took my arm, and as we walked out of the house into the sunshine she told me with tears in her eyes that they now had to have some help in the garden. She quickly recovered, and as we chatted she seemed to draw strength from the birds, the flowers and the sunshine. Although no longer actively involved in any local organisation, she seemed still to know about everything that was going on in the village and was well up-to-date with all the gossip.

As high summer passed and the days started perceptibly to shorten, Margery's spirits seemed to decline further. On the day when the swallows gathered for the last time on the telegraph poles prior to their departure *en masse* for warmer climes, she sighed a deep sigh, as if her whole being suddenly sensed that she would not be in her garden as she had been for decades past to welcome them and rejoice in their return.

Fortunately for her, Margery's death was not long in coming, for she could never have survived in an old people's home for very long. As it was, she was able to sit out in her conservatory during the golden days of late September and early October, watching her birds and rejoicing in the fuchsias, michaelmas daisies, golden rod, sedum and phlox which made her garden so colourful and still attracted bees and the autumn butterflies.

The Indian summer came and went all too quickly, but not before Margery had delighted at the arrival in her garden of an all-white blackbird - the first pure albino she had ever seen in a lifetime of studying ornithology and watching birds. Donald, who was now almost as interested in birds as his wife, immediately christened the blackbird 'Ermine' for, as he told me one day, its colour reminded him of the pure silky white of the ermine moths which were attracted by the lights in the kitchen window.

'It gives me a strange feeling of foreboding', Donald said to me one day as he told me all about Ermine.

'Why's that?'

'Well, John, one of the old villagers told me that the last time a white blackbird had been seen in the village was when Margery was born.'

The other birds in the garden saw Ermine as a threat and tried to chase him away, but such was the understanding Margery had with birds that she was able to calm them and at the same time, hobbling outside, call Ermine by name; whereupon he would follow her back into the conservatory, where she would feed him until he wanted no more.

One day in late November, Margery had asked Donald if she could sit out in the conservatory for just a few minutes. Against his better judgement - for it was a raw day with a cutting east wind - he agreed. He left her in her favourite armchair with a large travelling rug draped over her whilst he went through to the kitchen to make a cup of tea.

When he returned he spoke briefly to Margery, but there was no reply. She was dead. At her feet was the white blackbird, silent, with head cocked on one side, as he looked plaintively up at his mistress and benefactor.

91

'Do you know, John', Donald said to me when I called to see him the day before the funeral. 'I couldn't get Ermine out of that conservatory for two whole days - he wouldn't budge until the undertaker came to take Margery to the chapel of rest.'

As it was, the funeral had to be postponed. On the very day it was to be held, Donald was found dead in his bed by relatives who had called to see him before the church service. The doctor gave four different causes of death on the certificate, but the whole village decided that he had simply died of a broken heart.

I have seen many full congregations at village churches over the years, for country people still turn out in force to pay their last respects to one of their number, but I don't remember attending one with quite so many there. They were even overspilling into the churchyard. It was of course a double funeral, and Donald and Margery would I think have appreciated the service at the church with which they had been associated for so many years. Particularly poignant was the singing of Margery's favourite hymn:

'Morning has broken like the first morning,
Blackbird has spoken like the first bird.'

As I joined in the hymns and prayers, and listened to an excellent address by the vicar, I reflected on the couple's long and illustrious lives: Donald, wise and thoughtful, teacher, organiser and committee man *par excellence*, gardener extraordinaire, friend and mentor to so many; and Margery, doctor, philosopher, counsellor, ornithologist supreme and one of the kindliest women I had ever known. I thought, too, about their long and happy life together, and of their outstanding service to their village community. How they would be missed. As I joined the rest of the congregation for the interment in the churchyard, the vicar began intoning the dreadful but yet magnificent words of the Anglican burial service: 'Earth to Earth, Ashes to Ashes, Dust to Dust'. Suddenly the sky above was filled with birds of every description, and the mourners were treated to a concert of birdsong the like of which I have never heard before or since. It was as though every bird in the vicinity was there to join in the prayers to friends they had known for so long. As I looked up, marvelling at the sight and sound

of so many birds, there was a flutter of wings just beside me as a solitary bird flew down, landed and hopped around the edge of the double grave. It was the white blackbird. The funeral service ended, and as if by a signal the birds suddenly flew away in the wind, singing joyously as they did so, welcoming the spirits of Donald and Margery now freed from mortal shackles and soaring upwards like a pair of curlews in spring. Only the white blackbird remained. I was later told by villagers that it stayed there for three whole days and nights before flying away, never to be seen in Fordingley again.

93

Sort of a Cricket Person

My old friend and mentor Major Bunn had a way of describing people by referring to their particular interests in life. Thus the famous English artist John Constable was 'a painting fella', his military chums were 'army wallahs', his friend and eminent entomologist Professor Mortimer Sewell was 'a butterfly man' and our mutual acquaintance Franklin Elders, bookshop proprietor extraordinaire and demon googly bowler, was a 'sort of a cricket person'.

The major also had a nice line in understatement. He once confessed to a young journalist the 'he had played a little tennis and golf' when he had in fact been a county tennis player and a scratch golfer. In the same way, those of us who knew Franklin Elders smiled when we heard him described as a 'sort of a cricket person'. The truth was that Franklin lived every minute of his life for cricket, either on the field or through books on the sport. For many years I had known this remarkable character and legend of the local cricket scene. I spent untold happy hours talking to him about the game at his curiously-shaped old bookshop, which was situated in one of Denley's many alleys which we locals have always called 'ginnels'.

Franklin was actually born in Leeds immediately after the First World War, the youngest of four sons of a leading surgeon in the city. It cannot by all accounts have been easy for him growing up, for his three brothers were all brilliant high-fliers: two went up to Cambridge, were rugger blues and became leading Harley Street consultants, whilst the third won a scholarship to Oxford where he read classics and ultimately became a QC.

Franklin's parents not unnaturally expected their youngest son to aspire to the same glittering prizes and, when he turned out to possess no academic ability whatsoever, they were surprised and disappointed, and could not help themselves comparing him unfavourably with his high-flying brothers.

In fact, Franklin showed only two discernible interests in life from a very early age. The first was cricket and the second was books. He completely neglected his school studies, spending hours and hours with his friends practising his batting strokes, and the googly and leg-break bowling for which he was later to be famed in local cricket. He quite literally lived, ate and slept cricket, and his exasperated parents just did not know what to make of their youngest son.

'I really don't know what he's going to do or what's to become of him', his father remarked to friends one day. 'I suppose he might play for Yorkshire.'

Franklin might indeed have played for Yorkshire, but the Second World War happened at the wrong time. He was wounded in action and not fully fit to play until five years after the war ended. In any case he had by this time a bookshop to run, a shop he had only just acquired before war broke out.

Franklin had realised whilst still at school that he could not play cricket all the time. There was after all the winter, and wet days in summer. So when he was not able to be outside on the cricket field or in the nets, he was reading and developing his second great passion in life - books. It was when he was appointed school librarian that he suddenly knew what he really wanted to do in life, apart from playing his favourite summer game - run a bookshop.

To his parent's dismay he left school at the age of sixteen without any qualifications. After five years doing a rather unsatisfactory job as an assistant librarian in Bradford, his opportunity came. On his twenty-first birthday he was able - with a chance inheritance from his grandfather - to buy the business and living accommodation of a secondhand furniture shop in Denley, which he could readily convert to the purpose he had in mind. Although it was by no means the sort of career his parents intended for him, their reaction to his plan was one of philosophical resignation.

'If you're sure it's what you really want', his father said to him.

'I'm sure', replied Franklin, and he was.

Unfortunately, just as Franklin bought the shop, war broke out and he was called up. Cricket and books had to wait. It was a different world to which Franklin returned after the war. He had, moreover, suffered a serious leg injury; it was some time before it was sufficiently healed for him to play cricket, and even then he was left with a slight limp which destroyed his hopes of a first-class career in the game. It was as well that Franklin was not envious of his high-flying brothers, and was quite happy to settle for a more modest life as a bookshop proprietor in a small Dales market town.

It was in the early 1950s when, as a cricket-mad schoolboy myself, I first met Franklin at his shop. We talked about the game for hours. One memorable day he took me into a special room at the end of the shop, a room which was not open to the general public, and showed me his private collection of cricket books and memorabilia, a collection he had started as a schoolboy and which was his pride and joy.

I whistled out loud as my eyes raced across famous cricket titles over the years, stopping to rest on what looked to be a complete set of *Wisden*. Franklin anticipated my questioning look.

'No, not quite a full set, John. I've just the 1916 edition to get. Very difficult to find, that one. You see it was in the war, and it's particularly scarce because it included the obituaries of leading cricketers killed on the Western Front and was quickly sold out to their grieving relatives.'

Now there are in my experience two distinct and very different kinds of second-hand bookshops. The first is one where the books on the shelves are all beautifully arranged, the different subjects are all clearly and concisely labelled in their own sections, and the authors are set out in alphabetical order. Such shops alway remind me of certain homes I have visited, where everything has its proper place and are immaculately furnished, spotlessly clean and so tidy that one hardly likes to sit down on the settee for fear of ruffling a cushion! In such a shop, one fears taking a book from its shelf.

The second type of bookshop is right at the opposite end of the spectrum, and is more akin to a battlefield or to the bedroom of a teenage daughter. It has been said that when you look at the father of a teenage daughter you are looking at a man who is not fully in control of his own destiny! I feel rather like that when I enter this particular type of bookshop, with dirt- and dust-covered books strewn across floors and jammed into shelves with no regard to order, author or subject matter. Around the dark recesses at the far end of such a shop are stacks of unsorted books gathering dust, and to ask the proprietor whether he has a particular book in stock is an unproductive exercise. It is, I have often reflected, rather like a visit to modern-day Beirut where, without a survival kit which should preferably include a compass, your return from the darker and more hidden recesses cannot be guaranteed!

Franklin's shop quite definitely fell into the 'battlefield' category, and it is his shop and others like it which tend to linger in the memory. Books on a shelf tend to carry for me the same sort of memories as plants in my garden. I have an unusual deep-red hydrangea which was given to me by an old gardener in Leeds known simply as 'Jack' by all who knew him, pinks given to me by friends in Sussex, and a clump of white michaelmas daisies, descendants of a gift to my Scottish granny by her milkman over forty years ago. Similarly, when I look at my books nearly every one has a story to tell: a special gift, an inheritance or a purchase from a 'battlefield'-type bookshop, reminding me of their rather eccentric proprietors in different parts of the country.

To describe Franklin as an eccentric would possibly be unfair to him, but that he was a 'character' was not in doubt. For a start he never showed the slightest interest in the financial side of running a business. His parents could never come to terms with this lamentable truth, but the fact was that as long as his shop provided what he needed in life - which was not much - he was perfectly happy.

Franklin lived for his cricket and his books. His knowledge of the latter was by no means restricted to his almost encyclopaedic memory for just about everything which had ever been written on the subject of his favourite summer game. As a teenager - particularly when he had been school librarian - he had devoured all the recognised classics, had ploughed through Dickens, delighted in Shakespeare and Chaucer, knew most of the great English poets and had since acquired a passable knowledge of novels and modern first editions.

Of course it is not possible for a bookshop proprietor to know everything in such an enormous field, but Franklin knew more than most. Whenever I went into Franklin's shop - which was as frequently as I could - I never ceased to be amazed at his incredible all-round knowledge, based I suppose on his wide reading as a teenage librarian, during the time spent convalescing and recovering from his war wounds, and on the information he had picked up from dealers and customers over the years.

On my visits to his shop I always asked if I could go into his 'cricket room' to view his prize collection of books and memorabilia. He kept very few cricket books for sale because most of them tended to end up in his own private collection. What particularly struck me was how many books he had concerning Yorkshire County Cricket Club, including a complete run of the club's yearbooks. Like all true tykes, Franklin followed the fortunes of Yorkshire very seriously indeed. He had been to all the county grounds - Headingley, Bradford Park Avenue, Sheffield, Harrogate, Scarborough, Middlesborough and Hull - and to all the test match grounds. He must often have reflected, I thought, that but for his war injuries he might himself have graced those wickets.

And always on such occasions when I left the shop, his parting shot would be:

'I'm still looking for the 1916 *Wisden*; you'll let me know if you come across it, John, you promise.'

'I promise', I would always reply.

When it came to actually playing the game, Franklin was very interesting to watch. His style completely overcame the physical disabilities which had left him with a limp and a shortened left arm. His was a most graceful classical batting style. His late cut was reminiscent of the great Cyril Washbrook and his cover drive was elegant in the fashion of Tom Graveney. His bowling was as unorthodox as his batting was orthodox. He specialised in leg break and googly bowling, modelled on his hero Doug Wright of Kent and England fame.

He played his cricket not for Denley but by his own choice for the small village of Farthinghope, which lay just two or three miles lower down the dale, and he did so for no better reason than that the Fox and Hounds at Farthinghope was his 'local', where he had been accepted as 'one of them'. By happy chance his great friend from boyhood, Geoffrey Bateman, headmaster of the village school, also turned out for the team and they became famous throughout the district for their bowling combination. Franklin bowled his leg breaks and googlies from the pub end, and at the churchyard end Geoffrey bowled slow left arm in a style reminiscent of the Yorkshire county player Johnny Wardle - orthodox round-the-wicket stuff with the odd 'chinaman' being thrown in to keep the batsmen guessing.

Through the 1950s and 1960s Franklin and Geoffrey were famed throughout the district for this combined attack. As the art of spin bowling gradually went out of fashion, they became even more successful, since younger players, with no practice against spin, found themselves completely baffled when they came to face these two wily compaigners. All they knew was how to play fast and medium-paced bowling, so when they suddenly had to face two experienced spin-bowlers, whose accurate line and length had been fashioned by hours of practice with each other during their formative years, they were completely bamboozled. Their accuracy was such that they could each with regularity pitch the ball onto a pocket handkerchief placed at the batsman's end of the wicket. Spectators particularly used to chuckle when young batsmen, who clearly had a high opinion of themselves and fancied their chances of knocking the two 'old men' all over the ground, found themselves totally unable to judge which way the ball was going to spin, particularly the 'wrong-uns' in the form of Franklin's googlies and Geoffrey's 'chinamen'.

Franklin and Geoffrey made an interesting batting combination too, with the former's classical style contrasting rather oddly but very effectively with the latter's slogging. Bowlers found it difficult to adjust to their very different styles; an exquisite late cut at one end would be followed by a haymaker at the other end.

Franklin and Geoffrey could possibly have played on for quite a few years, but after their performance in the last match of the season against Upper Wasdale they decided to 'quit while they were ahead'. Franklin told me later that this match was for him the culminating success in a lifetime of cricketing enjoyment.

Upper Wasdale had won the toss and elected to bat on the sort of late summer's day which epitomises the image of English village cricket. The sun was shining out of a cloudless blue sky, which blended perfectly with the green of the cricket field and the whites of the players. The scattering of spectators around the boundary fence relaxed whilst the poplar trees at the churchyard end swayed slightly in the gentle breeze; bees were murmuring, birds were singing, grasshoppers were clicking in the adjoining meadow and the sound of the nearby river, still running in spate after a recent thunderstorm, could be heard in the distance.

When Franklin and Geoffrey were eventually brought on to bowl, Upper Wasdale were 100 without loss, going strongly and coping easily with Farthinghope's young lads who fancied themselves as fast bowlers. When at last the captain of the home team brought 'the old men' on to bowl, the transformation was immediate and dramatic. Franklin and Geoffrey seemed inspired: their bowling, which had been honed and crafted over the years, reached perfection that lovely summer afternoon. Upper Wasdale's young batsmen thought they could dispatch the deceptive slow bowling to all corners of the ground, but in attempting to knock the cover off every ball they missed the spin over and over again. Upper Wasdale were all out for

100

150. Geoffrey's figures were 5 for 40, and Franklin took the remaining 5 wickets at a cost of just 10 runs.

As a compliment to their bowling effort, the home captain sent Franklin and Geoffrey in to open Farthinghope's innings. Their batting turned out to be just as inspired as their bowling. In short, they knocked off the 151 runs required to win in double-quick time, Franklin's classical style and Geoffrey's slogging quickly taking their team to victory.

It was after the match that they both instinctively decided it was the right moment to retire.

'As good a time as any', said Franklin to his friend.

When Franklin hung up his cricket boots after his epic performance against Upper Wasdale, he devoted himself more enthusiastically than ever to his bookshop, his collection of cricket books and memorabilia, and to his by now almost obsessive search for a 1916 *Wisden*.

Whenever I went into his shop he would always let me into his 'holy of holies', where my eyes would feast again on his wonderful collection of memorabilia: autographs, programmes, score cards, signed miniature cricket bats and photographs. But it was his books which were his pride and joy, and which he liked to talk about more than anything - particularly *Wisdens*, whose buff and yellow covers evoked for him memories of seasons and names long past, his bible of cricketing facts.

'Did you know, John, that the early *Wisdens* were not just about cricket - I think in those days John Wisden had a job to fill the book with cricket statistics. You can learn a lot in those editions about church festivals, the varsity boat race and even the state of Anglo-Chinese relations.'

I listened intrigued as he continued.

'Talk about Kerry Packer being cricket's first entrepreneur - did you know that Wisden had a sports shop, went into business with Fred Lillywhite, the publisher of the *Young Cricketer's Guide* and arranged commercial cricket matches in the 1850s? His idea was that his 'Almanack' would be not only a lucrative publishing venture but it would also extend the memory of his own name among cricket followers.'

Franklin carried on talking as he started lovingly going through the different editions on his shelves.

'Look at this, John', he said, taking out the 1884 edition. 'You can read all about the smokers versus non-smokers match played at Lords. And what about this', he went on, picking out the volume from 1896. 'This was the first clothbound edition - cost two bob - quite a lot of money in those days. Don't think crowd trouble is anything new, John', he said as he opened the pages of the 1907 edition, and read out:

'Some sections of the spectators walked right across the pitch and inflicted some damage, noticeable at one end, causing the match to be abandoned'.

'Interesting isn't it?' he said, as my expression registered some surprise.

'Pessimism about the game isn't anything new either', he continued as he picked out the 1914 *Wisden*, where the editor commented: "It is impossible to take other than a gloomy view with regard to the immediate future of cricket".'

By this time Franklin was really into his stride talking about his favourite subject, and we read and talked together of the 1932 edition which described the famous or infamous 'bodyline' series against the Aussies, the 1938 edition describing Len Hutton's epic innings of 364 and many, many more.

I often reflected during my visits to Franklin's shop that cricket and literature have been closely linked ever since the game assumed qualities and characteristics familiar to every devotee of the summer game. Certainly no other sport has so many accounts of colourful tours and players.

I visited Franklin's shop many times over the years. We always talked of cricket and cricket books. We discussed that doyen of cricket writers, Sir Neville Cardus, and his lyrical essays on the summer game. Cardus was one of his favourites, along with C C R James and his famous book *Beyond the Boundary*, and of course the great W G Grace's 1891 book on cricket. Among modern writers he liked John Arlott, Jim Swanton and of course J M Kilburn on the history of Yorkshire County Cricket Club. But our talk inevitably came back to *Wisden*, and I would always ask him whether he had found the 1916 edition yet. He would shake his head and say.

'One day, John. One of these fine days.'

In truth it was not for want of trying, for over the years he had made repeated and strenuous attempts to get hold of it, but it had continued to elude him. In his early years at the bookshop it had actually been offered to him on several occasions, but he was not prepared to pay what he then considered an exorbitant price. There were other times when he had been outbid at auction, and times, too, when he had seen it advertised only to be told when he telephoned that it had already been sold.

The time eventually came when Franklin decided to sell his shop and retire. He decided to invite some of his special friends and customers to drinks at his shop to mark the occasion. It was a splendidly enjoyable event in a thoroughly anarchic way. We were all browsing around, drinks in hand, as we pushed up against the shelves and each other whilst trying desperately hard not to trip up over piles of books and packages. It was a scene of delightful chaos - even more chaotic than was customary in Franklin's shop.

I tried to get away from the suffocating crowd as I barged, pushed and jumped my way to the very back of the shop. Here I started to look through some of the stock in between taking repeated sips of a rather splendid vintage claret. In the very furthest and darkest corner I stumbled over yet another box of unsorted books. Out of curiosity I started to go through them. I noticed that the books at the bottom of the pile dated from around the First World War. The books right at the very bottom made me drop my empty glass: here was a complete set of *Wisden* from 1914 to 1918.

I slowly made my way back to the front of the shop, carrying the 1916 *Wisden* behind my back, and eventually found Franklin.

'Marvellous party, Franklin', I said, 'and do you know I've found a book I'd like to buy from that boxed lot at the back of the shop.'

'I'm surprised you've found anything of interest there, John', he replied. 'It's a boxed lot I bought for a song at a saleroom yesterday. I haven't gone through it yet but I doubt if there's much there. I've never been able to resist "boxed lots" - you never know what might turn up. It's the proverbial lucky dip in the old bran tub.'

'I think you might find this of interest. How much do you want for it?'

As his eyes looked upon the familiar-coloured cricketing almanack dated 1916, Franklin's face was a mixture of surprise, amazement, delight and sheer astonishment.

'Well, who'd have believed it', he said eventually. 'I often dreamed of finding it at a church bazaar or jumble sale, but to find it in a boxed lot on the very last day in my own shop, well it's absolutely unbelieveable. The 1916 *Wisden* at last - I'll really be able to enjoy my retirement now.'

I couldn't resist reminding him of my question.

'How much do you want for it, Franklin?'

'Oh, I've just decided it's not for sale', he said laughing.

'I thought you might', I replied as I laughed with him.

'Another glass of wine, John?'

Fred's Allotment

One of the glories of English village life is the diversity of the characters living in them, and the village of Farthinghope boasted quite a number outside its cricket team, for whom Franklin Elders played with such distinction.

Fred Digby was certainly a totally different character from Franklin in every way possible. For a start he had no 'book learning' as he would call it. In truth I doubt if he had ever read a book in his whole life. Nor did he play cricket.

He had left school as soon as he could and, like his father and grandfather before him, had gone to work on the railways. Any spare time he could lay his hands on was spent in his allotment, a quarter acre plot adjacent to the main street which ran through the village. Fred worked on the railways until the early 1960s, when Lord Beeching closed railway lines and stations all over the country. Fred gave a warning then to anyone who was prepared to listen that it was one of the most disastrous and short-sighted political decisions ever made - except that he didn't put it in quite those words!

'They'll cum tae rue it', he was heard to say in the local pub in what was undoubtedly one of his politer reflections on the subject of railway closures.

Many a time in the years that have followed I have reflected, as I have battled along our traffic-congested roads, just how right my old railway-worker friend was.

Fortunately, from Fred's point of view, he had just reached retirement age when his local station and branch line were closed. More importantly still, he was able to devote himself wholeheartedly to his beloved allotment. By the time I first came to know Fred, which was when I called to take a statement from him regarding a disputed right of way, his family had long since grown up and left home, he had retired, and as he put it:

'It's jus' t' missus an' me, like, now.'

It was at his allotment where we first met, and we soon fell into talk about gardening, plants, flowers and vegetables as soon as we had finished the business in hand.

In appearance Fred always reminded me of Adam the gardener in the *Sunday Express*. His frame was rather bent after a lifetime of work on the railways. He wore real old-fashioned leather boots, shabby corduroy trousers, an old moth-eaten brown windcheater, and a shirt with a collar stud at the top. His face underneath the silvery hair which protruded from his habitual cloth cap was weather-beaten, and there was always a good strong briar pipe between his lips. He looked exactly what he was - an old-fashioned 'muck and magic' gardener, whose success lay not in science or modern methods but plain, honest hard work and years of experience.

Fred's conversation was Yorkshire, very Yorkshire. He didn't waste words and had a nice line in understatement which has been forever the hallmark of a Dalesman's wit.

'Bit parky today, lad', he would say to me on a perishing cold day when I would be thinking more on the lines of brass monkeys.

Or 't' weathers turned old-fashioned', when he was faced with twelve feet of snow; and when there was a howling gale, his choice of adjective was invariably 'draughty'.

Whenever I met Fred and asked how he was keeping, his reply was always:

'Middlin', lad, jus' middlin'.'

I couldn't ever get him to admit to being 'Fair to middlin''. He explained to me once how it was that he always gave this reply:

'Ah were at t' allotment society meetin' once ovver. Ah 'eard one o' t' members ask t' chairman o' t' meetin', Jack, 'ow 'e were doin', like - this were by way o' conversation afore t' job were started, like - an' Jack said "Ah've nivver felt fitter in me life". Ah'd cause tae remember them words, 'cos a week after he said 'em, like, Jack were dead. 'E'd jus' dropped down dead in 'is garden, like, an' that were it. Now tha knows why Ah nivver lets on 'ow Ah'm feelin' like. Best jus' tae say "middlin"', Ah reckons.'

There is another saying which I shall always associate with Fred. 'It's black ovver t' wife's mother's', he would say whenever there were storm clouds in the distance. It was an expression which in Fred's case was used with some feeling, for he had been the target of his mother-in-law's rudeness, sarcasm and hostility for years - a hostility undoubtedly born from the fact that she disapproved of her daughter's marriage to a man who was not of the social standing she would have chosen for her offspring.

Fred's wife Doris owed a good deal to her mother's influence. A tall, gaunt woman, she was without question the boss at home. Her house was kept immaculately tidy; her housekeeping was based on a daily routine which would not suffer interruption, and meals were always served on the dot. Although Doris was happy enough to welcome the splendid produce which came from the allotment all through the year, the house was her domain and Fred was expected to do exactly as he was told. She made him take his boots off outside the back door, he wasn't allowed to smoke his pipe indoors, and it was a criminal offence for him to be late for meals.

It was no wonder that Fred sought refuge in his allotment, for as he was fond of saying:

'A man's got tae 'ave sumwheer tae go, tha knows.'

Fred's allotment was not, like his health, 'jus' middlin''. It was quite superb.

It was divided into two distinct parts. The main area was devoted to the growing of traditional vegetables: potatoes, carrots, peas, runner beans, french beans, cabbage, cauliflowers, broccoli, parsnips, parsley, leeks, onions, shallots, lettuce, radishes and celery, marrows on an old muck heap and a couple of rows of sweet peas thrown in to add a splash of colour. The other area, at the end nearest the village main street, was Fred's pride and joy - a truly amazing display of polyanthus and pansies, all the better for being in the partial shade of two old greengage trees, the flowers contrasting with the traditional allotment vegetables behind them.

When it came to growing vegetables, Fred's methods were entirely traditional, originally handed down to him by his father and perfected by years of experience.

To say that Fred was a believer in 'muck' would be a considerable understatement. There always seemed to be a heap of well-rotted manure waiting to be dug in or actually in the process of being dug in. Fred knew alright that farmyard muck lightens the soil and keeps its texture open, and he also knew the value of wood ash from his bonfires and soot from his chimney which he always swept himself. Perhaps he didn't realise that wood ashes contain potash and soot contains ammonia, but he knew very well how beneficial they both were for his plants. Fred was proud of his compost heap, too. Nothing from home or garden ever went to waste: household scraps, vegetable refuse, leaves - everything went in till it was 'reight good stuff' as Fred called it.

He also believed in what he called 'muckwatter', which as I remember was simply farmyard drainings diluted with three times as much water and which he applied at about three gallons a square yard.

This holy trinity of farmyard manure, compost and 'muckwatter' was undoubtedly the basis of Fred's success as an allotment gardener. Years of this treatment resulted in the best and richest loamy black soil I have ever seen. It was what gardeners call 'friable' - no lumps, no clay, just beautiful soil which crumbled in the hand.

The rows and rows of vegetables were set out in almost military formation, but, being a Yorkshireman, Fred didn't like to waste an inch of ground. His 'catch' crops were better than most people's vegetable gardens. There was spinach and lettuce between his cauliflowers, sprouts between his beans and dwarf early peas between his celery. When it came to the rotation of crops, Fred knew from years of experience that peas should not follow beans, celery should not follow carrots and chives should not follow leeks or onions. Pests and diseases never stood a chance on Fred's allotment. He changed his crops around so frequently and skilfully that they were never able to establish themselves anywhere.

I learnt how to dig properly from watching my boyhood mentor, countryman and friend 'owd Jacob', and his friend and fellow allotment holder Fred Digby reminded me of him when I called to see him at work in his hallowed plot of soil.

It was always the back end of the year when Fred went to work. He knew that digging should be completed before the soil was too wet, for if it was left until spring the soil would be deprived of the beneficial actions of air, rain and frost through the long northern winter.

I shall always remember calling to see him one golden October day. He started the job by marking the ground into strips about ten inches wide, for he knew very well that if the trenches were longer than the one dug then it would be difficult to keep the soil level. Next he took out a trench about a spade wide and a spade deep, cut the sides of this trench straight and square, and removed the loose earth from the bottom. Then he removed the soil from the trench to the other end of the ground to be dug over.

Another trench of the same size was then taken out, the soil transferred into the first trench, and broken up by cutting and beating with the spade.

I watched in wonder as the process continued until the whole area was dug over, the last trench taken out being filled with soil taken from the first trench. All the time Fred was manuring the area by throwing muck with his fork along the bottom of the trenches and throwing soil from the next trench on top of it.

I knew better than to interrupt whilst Fred was digging, but I didn't want to anyway, for to watch him at work was an education in itself. Eventually he straightened himself, put on his moth-eaten brown

windcheater, stood back to look over his work with a critical eye, lit his pipe and said to me:

'That'll do, lad. It'll not tek any fault, Ah reckons.'

Fred knew the art of digging right enough, and it was from this solid base that his row upon row of prizewinning vegetables were cultivated. But this in his eyes was just bread and butter gardening. The 'jam' - his pride and joy - took the form of the large bed of polyanthus and pansies under the partial shade of the greengage trees.

Now the primula family, of which the polyanthus is a member, is found all over the world from the Himalayas to the Rockies, but especially in Asia. It might be thought that taking a plant from Siberia or the Alps - where there is a long winter rest and a slow change to growing conditions - to Yorkshire - where the seasons are not so sharply defined and where there can be snow even in June - would be doomed to failure, but the magnificent display in Fred's allotment proved conclusively that it is a plant which adapts pretty well.

I always knew that spring had arrived in Farthinghope when I saw Fred's polyanthus and pansies in full flower. I never ceased to be amazed at the wide variety of colours. This variety is surprising when you realise that the polyanthus is a cross between the cultivated primrose and the cowslip, and was originally only coloured white and yellow. Lots of different colours have been developed from the original strains of eighty-five years ago, and the old florist's polyanthus with red and blue petals have come back into favour along with other flowers associated with the Victorian era.

Fred's success with his flowers as well as his vegetables was based on sound and intuitive preparation. His polyanthus plants grew on a good bed liberally supplied with leaf mould, well-rotted muck and bone meal, and when he'd swept his chimneys he reckoned that his pansies always benefited from a dressing of soot. Fred, like all true countrymen, thought that gardening should not be for appearance but for pleasure and the kitchen. His vegetables were for the kitchen and his flowers strictly for pleasure. It was a pleasure he shared with the whole village, for, being situated right next to the main street,

112

Fred's allotment was a continual source of comment, discussion, admiration and affection.

The years passed and there were many changes in the village, but Fred's allotment never changed: the rows of prizewinning vegetables and the glorious display of pansies and polyanthus, a seemingly never-changing landmark which distinguished Farthinghope from the adjoining villages and hamlets.

Then one spring day, Fred arrived home one Saturday after working all day in his allotment to find his wife Doris dead. She had collapsed and died of a massive stroke. There had been no warning and no time to prepare for such a shock.

Fred carried on as best he could, but things did not seem the same without his lifelong partner. He missed her in all sorts of ways, even the fact that she was not there to tell him to take his boots off before coming into the kitchen and warning him not to smoke his pipe indoors.

If it hadn't been for his allotment I doubt whether Fred would have survived the death of his wife for very long. He was fortunate, too, that his widowed sister Mary lived only two miles away in Denley and was able to help him with domestic chores. Fred and Mary had always got on well together, and everyone thought it an excellent idea when they decided to pool their resources under the same roof. Fred left his own rented cottage and went to live with his sister in Denley. The move was to prove his undoing.

Soon after Fred's move, rumours began to circulate in the village that the local council had its eyes on the site of Fred's allotment for a block of old people's flats. Fred had never taken much notice of village gossip and so didn't pay any attention to the talk about the allotment, until one day out of the blue he received a letter from the council asking if he was prepared to exchange his allotment for one in Denley which had become vacant.

'Ah'm not budgin' for them or anyone else', he said defiantly. 'It's tekken more than fifty year tae mek a reight job o' yon place, an' Ah'm not startin' all ovver agin sumwheer else at my age.'

He heard no more from the council for a while after that, but talk continued in the village that the council was still desperately keen to get hold of Fred's allotment to build some flats.

One day late the same year I was working in my office when my secretary Clare interrupted me to say that Fred was in reception and had to see me straight away. I knew immediately that it must be something important, for Fred and I usually conducted business at his allotment where we both felt comfortable. He had never been to my office before.

'Show him in straight away', I said to Clare.

I have seen many distressed and anxious people over the years, but I shall never forget the expression on Fred's face as he handed over to me a notice to quit he had received from the council, and said quietly:

'They've signed me bloody death warrant, lad.'

As I looked at Fred's despairing face and read the notice, I racked my brains to see what - if anything - I knew or could remember about allotments and the law relating to them. I had of course advised clients on many occasions on notices to quit in respect of farms, smallholdings, houses, flats and business premises, but this was the first time I had even seen one relating to an allotment. Was there any way I could help my old friend?, I wondered.

As I looked upon Fred's questioning face, with an expression which sought reassurance and comfort, I quickly realised how little I knew about the subject. I knew that, during the nineteenth century, allotments were provided for cultivation by poor and industrious parishioners, and as recreation grounds for parishioners under certain Poor Law and Enclosure Acts and by appropriation of parochial charity lands for that purpose. I guessed that Fred's allotment was probably a 'field garden' given to what used to be termed 'the labouring poor' and would originally have been managed by wardens - the vicar, churchwardens and two ratepayers - in the days before these responsibilities were transferred to the local council. I also knew that, in ordinary circumstances, the compulsory acquisition of an allotment could only happen if suitable land was offered in exchange. What I didn't know, and had to keep Fred waiting whilst

I looked it up in our law library, was that an allotment holding can be ended if it can be shown that the holder of the allotment resides one mile or more outside the parish. In such a case, a notice to quit can be served followed by an application for possession in the local county court.

As I read the law, and compared it with the notice Fred had received, I sighed to myself at the prospect of telling Fred that there was no legal way of fighting the council. Fred must have known as I returned to my office that there was nothing I could do to help him. The expression on my face must have said it all. Fred slowly got up, moved to the door and turned briefly to face me as he repeated:

'Like Ah said, they've signed me bloody death warrant.'

Fred did not live to see his beloved allotment repossessed or the rather ugly block of old people's flats built on the loamy, fertile soil which had been his lifetime's work. He died a week later. His death certificate contained a number of technical medical terms, but to me the cause of his death was simple enough. He had died of a broken heart, unable to face a future without his wife and the allotment which was all he had to live for after her death.

Fred's sister, who came to see me after his funeral, was distraught.

'It's all my fault, Mr Francis', she said. 'If I hadn't suggested he moved in with me, this would never have happened.'

'You really mustn't blame yourself', I replied. 'If I didn't know about this particular law, you couldn't possibly have known. If anyone's to blame, it's me.'

A couple of years after Fred's death, I was in Farthinghope, so I stopped on the main street and looked at the ugly brick-built block of flats. I shuddered. I closed my eyes and saw in memory the rich loamy soil, the rows of prizewinning vegetables, and the colourful bed of pansies and polyanthus - all gone now, along with the old gardener responsible for them. As I stood there and contemplated this melancholy scene, I recalled some words from the preamble to the Allotment Act of 1832 which I had read in the office library when I had seen Fred for the last time: 'And whereas it would tend much to the welfare and happiness of the poor if allotments could be let at a fair rent and in small portions to industrious cottagers of good character ...'

Well, I reflected to myself, Fred was certainly an 'industrious cottager' of 'good character' and definitely a member of what the Victorians would have called 'the deserving poor'. He had been industrious, alright, in his lifetime of work on the railways and in his allotment. In fact Fred had little time or patience for able-bodied men who didn't work. He shared, I think, the view of Pericles in ancient Athens that 'there is no disgrace in poverty, the disgrace lies in not trying to escape from it'. As these thoughts went through my mind, I remembered a conversation I had with him one day on his allotment, when he was expressing strong views both on the idle rich and on young men who choose not to work.

'Aye, lad', he said in conclusion, 'there's drones at t' top and t' bottom, Ah reckons.'

As I turned away and took one last sad look at the site before returning to my car, I remembered something else Fred had said and said often over the years:

'A man's got tae 'ave sumwheer tae go.'

I realised that it was the prospect of its loss which had finally destroyed his will to live.

But, I finally reflected as I got back in my car, the allotment had not just been 'sumwheer tae go', nor had it been just a hobby, a place to grow lovely flowers and prizewinning vegetables, or even a way of escaping temporarily from a bossy wife. Nor was it just an oasis of peace where he could dig and plant, reap and sow, make the finest compost in Yorkshire and at the end of a day's work enjoy a quiet pipe.

Fred's allotment meant for him much more than all these things. It was in fact his life's work and everything he ever dreamed about: heartsease, nirvana, shangri-la, the crock of gold at the end of the rainbow . . . the promised land.

'Now This Deed Witnesseth . . .'

Lillian Fogarty lived in a purpose-built block of flats which I remembered being erected near to the centre of Denley in the 1960s. Hers was on the top floor, and from her lounge balcony she enjoyed a splendid view of the river running through the middle of the town and of the heather moors on the horizon.

I had met Lillian one evening when I had gone to give a talk to a local women's group, of which she was a member. We got into conversation over coffee afterwards, and as I was about to leave she asked if I would call round to see her some time to make a will for her. It was to be the first of many such visits, for she was one of those people who liked to alter her will about five or six times every year.

Lillian was a remarkable old lady in many different ways. She had reached a fairly senior position in the civil service before her retirement. It had been obvious to me at our first meeting that she was exceptionally knowledgeable, extremely well-read and possessed a brain which was still razor-sharp. It was also apparent, both from what she said and from the elegance and style of the flat furnishings, that she was what people used to call 'comfortably off'.

I knew that Lillian was an avid bridge player and was heavily involved in a number of local organisations in Denley. It was a waste of time trying to speak to her in the evening, for she seemed to be out every night! On my very first visit to her flat I quickly discovered another of Lillian's great interests in life. I rang the doorbell and after a minute or two she opened it. She hardly glanced up from the newspaper she was holding. Through large spectacles, attached to a chain around her neck, she was studying something in the paper with a rather puzzled and frustrated expression.

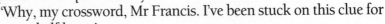

'Good morning, Mr Francis', she said. 'You've come at just the right moment. What's room for headbones in eight?'

'I'm sorry Miss Fogarty', I replied. 'I don't quite follow you.'

'Why, my crossword, Mr Francis. I've been stuck on this clue for the past half hour.'

Now I have never had much time or for that matter any inclination to spend on crosswords, partly I think because I live in the shadow of my mother and mother-in-law who are both experts, and partly because I live with the abiding memory of my old classics master Canon Peachey, who was a disappointed man on the rare occasion he failed to complete *The Times* crossword in the ten minute mid-morning break between Greek lessons.

'Room for headbones in eight', I repeated.

By sheer luck I had an inspired thought.

'How about scullery?'

'Of course', replied Lillian, 'of course. How stupid of me.'

'It's always easy when you know the answer', I said comfortingly.

It turned out to have been a great mistake on my part to have been lucky enough to answer Lillian's question. From that moment onward she regarded me as a crossword expert, a kindred spirit and an intellectual companion on the same wavelength, although in all truth I am very far from any of these.

Lillian's will had hardly been stored away safely in the wills cabinet before she summoned me to her flat to make some changes. I found on arrival that she expected me to help her finish the crossword again.

'Blisters to the TUC in five, Mr Francis?'

'Scabs, I should think', I replied without thinking.

Lucky again. Even though on my many subsequent visits I was never able to help her, on the strength of my first two fortuitously correct replies, Lillian regarded me as her consultant. If I could not help her finish her crossword, then it was quite clearly the fault of the compiler in dreaming up clues so contrived and obscure that even her visiting expert could not fathom them!

I sometimes used to think that Lillian's frequent will-changes were a device to get me to her flat so she could talk to me about her two favourite subjects, crosswords and bridge. The fact that I have never done crosswords regularly and that I have never played bridge in my life was no deterrent. My total ignorance did not prevent me from marvelling at her incredible memory as she talked about games and rubbers played in years gone by.

'Miriam opened with two hearts', she would say, describing the opening rubber at a particular congress, 'and Pauline made "no bid", Christine followed with three spades . . . '

By this time I was already lost, and became more and more confused as Lillian continued her detailed account, up to and including the moment she and her partners narrowly missed 'a grand slam'.

Fascinating though these lengthy accounts must have been to a bridge connoisseur, they were hardly the reason for my visits to Lillian. I always tried to steer her gently back to the subject of her will and the changes to it, which were the real reason for my presence.

Now the vast majority of wills I make are quite simple and straightforward affairs, but there are a few people, very often elderly ladies like Lillian, who choose to make exceptionally long wills containing a large number of small bequests to various relations, friends, neighbours, local organisations and charities. Lillian's will certainly fell into this category. The legacies under clause 3 started with '(a) To Denley Parish Church one hundred pounds' right through to '(v) To Denley Victim Support Scheme twenty-five pounds', with all manner of charities, groups, and individuals benefitting in between. Every time I made a new will for her, I wondered what I would do if Lillian had decided to make another four legacies and I had used up all the letters of the alphabet. Fortunately, she always seemed to delete as many legacies as she added, and at the same time she was forever making small changes to the amounts certain beneficiaries were to receive.

One day Lillian phoned me at the office and asked if I would call to see her. I assumed that it would be to discuss yet another alteration to her will, so I was surprised when she said:

'It's not my will this time, Mr Francis, it's about my flat. You know it's leasehold don't you? Well, the landlord's agent has called a meeting to discuss repairs and I need some advice before I go to it as to what exactly my responsibilities are.'

It was no surprise at all to learn that Lillian needed advice on this particular matter, for in my experience there is nearly always trouble in blocks of flats over maintenance, repairs and service charges. If there is a residents' committee, the members often fall out; and if in the case of leasehold flats the landlord's agent does the job, he often does it badly. There is usually a failure to obtain proper estimates, to make contingency plans and to set up a fund to cope with expensive repairs. The agent is often further handicapped by squabbles amongst the flat-owners as to who is to pay what, by the refusal of some to agree to anything being done and by others who leave their flats without paying their share.

In the case of the block of flats where Lillian lived, it had become increasingly obvious that substantial repairs had become necessary both externally and internally. There were over twenty different flats in the building; some had two outside walls, whilst others in the middle had only one. I knew that the first thing I needed to do when advising Lillian on the sharing out of the costs and her legal responsibilities was to look at her lease, so I asked her.

'I thought you'd want to see it, Mr Francis. Here it is. I hope you can understand it better than I can. I once tried reading it years ago but I couldn't make head nor tail of it.'

When I looked at the lease, I completely understood why even someone as intelligent and literate as Lillian had failed to understand it and had given up in despair. The lease, which had been prepared by a large city firm of solicitors in the 1960s, was fifty-three pages long and full of verbiage known to lawyers but a mystery to the non-legally qualified.

When I started my legal career as a very young, raw and inexperienced articled clerk, one of my first problems was being introduced to the mysteries of conveyances, mortgages, leases, wills, contracts, abstracts of title, requisitions and learning the meaning of legal expressions - words like 'demise', 'redendum' and 'habendum', 'And Whereas', 'And Reciting', 'Now This Deed Witnesseth'. Nowadays, legal documents are written in plainer and more modern English, although regrettably many are not much shorter. When I looked at Lillian's lease, its style, length and verbiage immediately took me back to the deeds and documents I struggled to understand during my early days.

I have always tended to believe throughout my career in the law that the longer the document, the less likely it is to cover the point in dispute. Time without number over the years I have looked at lengthy and verbose old deeds when asked to advise on boundary responsibilities, only to find that they are completely silent on this vital matter. Even more importantly, I have often found that where the actual area of ownership is in issue, there is a wholly inadequate plan, no plan at all or a description like 'bounded on the south by land now or formerly belonging to Fred Bloggs'. Such a description is useless if Fred Bloggs is dead!

Based on these unhappy experiences, I looked at Lillian's lengthy and wordy lease with some apprehension. It was a feeling which turned out to be well justified. I noted that her flat was stated 'to extend from the top of the floorboards to the underside of the ceiling timber joists'. Then I turned to the all-important repair and maintenance clause, and read that Lillian had covenanted:

'To keep the flat and every part thereof in tenantable repair throughout the term hereby granted and it is hereby declared and agreed that there is included in this covenant as repairable by the Tenant (including replacement whenever such becomes necessary) the windows of the flat and the ceilings and floors of and in the said flat the joists or beams on which the said floors are laid but not joists or beams to which the said ceilings are attached provided always that the Tenant shall not repair or replace any joist or beams on the said floors as laid without giving notice to the occupier of the flat immediately below . . . '

At this point a smile spread across my face. I remembered a case from my student days in which the position and extent of floor joists featured. It is strange how some cases linger in the memory whilst others are completely forgotten. At all events, rather like 1066 and the *Magna Carta*, I could not forget the tragi-comic case of *Sturge v Hackett*.

In the summer of 1957 a certain Lieutenant Colonel Hackett was the tenant of a first-floor flat in a manor house. There was a fine decorative cornice on the outside of this eighteenth century property, which was a magnet for birds - particularly house martins and sparrows. As the Court of Appeal was later to observe, the colonel was no bird lover and evidently did not believe in the old country superstition that if you drive martins away, you drive away your luck at the same time. Now the ceiling of the colonel's flat was fixed to the underside of the floor joists of the attic flat above, and the top of the decorative cornice on the outside wall was lower than the underside of the floor joists. At one point, below the lintels, which projected above the cornice, and between the moulding of the cornice and some wire netting, was a sparrow's nest. To destroy this nest the colonel stood on his verandah, lit a paraffin rag which he had attached to a stick and applied it to the bottom of the nest - which of course caught fire. A piece of straw from the nest blew into a crevice either in the cornice or in the roof, which it ignited. The whole mansion was soon ablaze.

Substantial damage was caused to other flats in the building and to the ground floor occupied by the colonel's landlord. Not surprisingly, the legal and insurance ramifications were considerable, and lengthy court proceedings ensued. Clearly the colonel had been guilty of negligence but the crucial question of his insurers liability hinged upon whether the fire started on premises belonging to him. The court's decision was that they were liable because the nest was below the level of the underside of the floor joists to which his ceiling was attached.

I smiled again as I read Lillian's lease with its references to joists and as I remembered the facts of *Sturge v Hackett*.

'What are you smiling about, Mr Francis?'

'I'm sorry - it was just that the mention of joists in your lease reminded me of a case which had a funny side to it. Talking of joists - are there any in these flats? Its always looked to me to be a concrete-framed building. All the flats will have prefabricated floor-units, surely?'

'Well, of course its a concrete-framed building, Mr Francis. I should have thought that was perfectly obvious to anyone who had seen it.'

'Did your solicitor ever look at your flat when he acted for you on your purchase?', I asked.

'No, he just asked me into his office to sign up. He went through the lease very quickly and I didn't really follow him most of the time', replied Lillian.

I could not help but chuckle to myself at the thought that two city lawyers, one acting for the owner of the flats and the other acting for Lillian, had been sitting in their offices, respectively preparing and considering a lengthy lease with its many references to joists and beams, when a simple inspection would have revealed that they were in fact dealing with a concrete-framed building. This thought reinforced my long-held belief that city solicitors are not quite the experts which their publicity brochures and advertising material suggest, or indeed which they clearly consider themselves to be. It is a belief which is not simply based on the fact that I am a country solicitor, with totally different values, motives, and methods, but on a number of practical experiences during my years in the law.

Very early on in my career, a leading firm of London solicitors acting for clients who were moving up north to take a hotel just outside Denley asked me to represent them and bid on their behalf at the auction sale to be held at the Denley Heifer. I discovered upon meeting them that their supposedly expert and certainly expensive London lawyers had been through the proposed contract with them in the most cursory manner and had failed to make proper enquiries on various matters of crucial importance. Jonathan and Evelyn subsequently became clients of mine - and very good ones too.

I have watched as more and more city firms have amalgamated, expanded, and recruited more and more staff to service the needs of their corporate clients, to the point where they seem no longer very interested in private clients. If the ordinary man or woman in the street is taken on by such solicitors, he or she is likely to be shunted around different 'specialist' departments according to whether a conveyance, a divorce or a will is required. There cannot be a personal relationship between solicitor and client in the traditional sense.

One of the most hopeful signs for the survival and future success of family solicitors in general practice lies in the steady flow to them of substantial private clients disillusioned by their treatment at the hands of city lawyers. There are many people who look for more than 'expertise' in their solicitor. They want someone they can get to know personally, can talk to and can trust, someone who does not suffer from tunnel vision but who can take a broad and sometimes critical view of his or her overall interests. In short they are looking for a solicitor who can do most jobs for them. They want an 'all-rounder'.

I don't suppose many city solicitors spend much time actually going out of their offices to look at properties their clients are buying and selling. If I had the time I would visit every single one, but as I haven't I have tried to developed an instinct for those where an inspection is essential. I well remember the time I went to look at a bungalow my old friend Eddie Holmes had set his heart on buying. There was nothing wrong with the property from a legal point of view, but I noticed that adjacent to the main bedroom was a large garage belonging to the house next door.

'Have you thought what it would be like', I asked, 'if your neighbour is a motor enthusiast or has teenage sons revving up their bikes in the garage late at night?'

Many years later, Eddie was to tell me that saving him from that particular purchase was the best job I had ever done for him. It had not even been legal advice, it had simply been a comment based on actually looking at the property.

'Well, Mr Francis, what do you advise me to say to the landlord's agent at the meeting?'

Lillian's question rapidly brought me back to the subject in hand.

'Well, Miss Fogarty, I think you should begin by asking him to explain what the repairing clause, with its references to non-existent beams and joists, actually means. I should love to be a fly on the wall when he reports back and asks the same question of the city solicitor who drew up the lease in the first place. Let me know what happens, won't you?'

When I left Lillian's flat I could no longer suppress my laughter and chuckled aloud all the way back to my office. Joists and beams in a concrete-framed building. I wouldn't forget that for a long time!

In fact I had not enjoyed such a good laugh about a city solicitor since the day one of their number pompously enquired what precise arrangements I proposed to hand over the keys of the property his client was buying. This actually consisted of twenty acres of prime grazing land.

'We don't lock up land in Yorkshire', was my succinct reply.

Stranger Than Fiction

Much of my work has been concerned with the mundane, the ordinary, the commonplace and the repetition of the office routine. There have, however, occasionally been experiences which have been strange indeed, and have defied the rational and logical approach which a lawyer normally brings to his work.

Although not a superstitious person by nature, neither do I believe in tempting fate, and I have always kept an open mind when confronted by stories of mystery and the unexplained. In fact since my boyhood I have been rather fascinated by ghost stories, extra-sensory perception and other phenomena which cannot be scientifically accounted for.

I was brought up in an old manor house which possessed, amongst many unusual features, a cellar with an ancient well in it, a secret back staircase, numerous creaking floorboards and a plumbing system which produced the strangest noises imaginable. In particular, the flushing of the upstairs lavatory resulted in a high-pitched gurgling sound which lingered for a while before changing suddenly to hollow and blood-curdling groans. In the middle of the night, these were noises to stir the imagination.

Even in broad daylight in the village, I thought of ghosts whenever I went on one of my favourite walks up Staircase Lane. Local legend had it that in bygone days a horseman, galloping away down the lane after losing heavily at gambling in a local hostelry, had been thrown from his horse and died. Villagers said that the sound of galloping hooves could still be heard. I sometimes felt on my walks along Staircase Lane that I could hear a galloping horse in the distance; or was it, I wondered later when safely back home, just schoolboy imagination?

We children often often played at 'ghosts' in the old manor house and made a special ghost train in the cellar - a tour which combined lurid and highly imaginative artwork with copious hanging black cotton and luminous paint. Our 'ghost' games were humorous rather than sinister, but I still feel guilty when I recall the occasion I crept up the back staircase late one night and frightened my young cousin Michael by appearing at his bedside dressed in a white sheet and wearing a hideous face-mask. It was no surprise at all when he next came to stay that his mother sent a note with him which simply read: 'No ghosts this year please'.

Ghosts featured, too, at Christmas time. We children all had to do individual 'turns' for the enjoyment of the grown-ups before everyone joined in the singing of Christmas carols. There was poetry and melody from the girls - usually, if I remember rightly, *Tiger, Tiger, burning bright*, or *Hiawatha* and *Greensleeves* beautifully and sweetly sung. From the boys there was often a recitation of *Albert the Lion* or *Three Ha' Pence a Foot* delivered in the best Stanley Holloway tradition, and for comedy there would be an impersonation of Wilfred Pickles, Al Read or Ken 'I won't take my coat off, I'm not stoppin'' Platt.

Finally, all the lights would be turned out save for a solitary candle, behind which I sat alone ready to tell the annual Christmas ghost story. Truth to tell, I cannot remember the details of my ghost stories but I do recall the main theme which never changed from year to year. It was one which revolved around the discovery in some dark and haunted place of what appeared to be a collection of very old bones, which after many a twist and turn were eventually revealed to be the bones of the Christmas turkey we had all just enjoyed!

I suppose that most of us, if we are entirely honest with ourselves, can recall moments in our lives when we are aware of rather strange feelings about certain events, places and conversations, a sense of *déja vu*: I have been here before, I know this place, I have been in this company previously, I have been through this conversation, I recognise this, I know what is going to happen next, I know exactly what he is about to say. Over the years I have encountered such feelings a few times - a recognition, a prescience which the rational would no doubt dismiss but which seems to me to have gone beyond the explanations of imagination, chance or coincidence.

The first such incident occurred very early on in my legal career. As a young articled clerk, I was sent out to serve a writ on a man I had never heard of in a town which I had previously never visited. I parked in the centre of town, and to my astonishment I found that I had no need to ask directions, for I had a picture of the street in my mind which drew me to it as if by a magnet. As I turned into the street the whole layout, the design of the houses, the pub at one end of it and the corner shop at the other were all familiar to me. I knew exactly where I was going, a strange feeling considering I had never been there before - or had I?

On another occasion some years later, I had a particularly vivid dream one night that a blue handwritten letter would be delivered to my office the next afternoon, signed by a lady called 'Anne' and containing an enquiry in neat, ladylike handwriting about a will held in my office. The following day I was away on business but called into the office just before it closed on my way home. By this time I had forgotten all about my dream, but was quickly and rather eerily reminded of it when my secretary Clare came in with a blue envelope in her hand.

'A lady delivered this earlier this afternoon', she said, 'and asked if I would give it to you.'

As Clare left me to read the letter, the eerie feeling which had come over me when I saw the blue envelope intensified. The letter, which contained a request for me to check whether my firm had in its custody the will of a certain gentleman, was signed by a lady whose christian name was Anne. To the best of my knowledge, I knew neither Anne nor the person who was the subject of her enquiry.

Even stranger than the incident of Anne and the blue envelope was another occasion early on in my career when a young woman called Jane Thomas came into my office. She was newly married, and at the time she and her husband Dave were living with her parents. She had called to ask if I would act for the two of them in the purchase of their first house. At this interview, Jane saw me alone. As she was leaving, the expression on her face told me that she was worried and preoccupied.

'Do you believe in fortune tellers?', she suddenly asked.

Now solicitors are asked many strange questions from time to time, but this was a new one on me.

I hesitated for a moment before making a somewhat equivocal reply.

'Well, I try to keep an open mind about fortune tellers, but I reckon that most of them are probably charlatans. May I know why you are asking me this question?'

'Well, you see Mr Francis', replied Jane, 'I haven't told anyone and I just had to say something to somebody about it. Last Saturday, Dave and I went on a day trip to Blackpool, and he persuaded me to have my fortune told on the Golden Mile. I can't remember the name of the old lady - Madame Rosalie or Mirabelle or something like that - anyway she was a real homely Lancashire woman. She spoke so fast that most of what she said is a complete blur, but towards the end she suddenly stopped in full flow and I asked what was the matter. She didn't reply straight away, and I became frightened and asked her if I was going to die.'

'No dear', she replied, 'I don't see your death but I can tell you that you're going to marry twice and have two children.'

'Well, Mr Francis, I came out of that fortune-teller's booth shaking a bit, as you can imagine. I couldn't tell Dave what I had been told and I haven't been able to stop thinking about it.'

I wouldn't worry about it if I were you', I said in my best reassuring tone of voice. 'I'm sure everything will work out fine.'

I thought no more about Jane and Dave, until two years later I read in the local paper that Dave had been killed in a tragic accident on the building site where he was working. Jane came in to see me and asked me to handle the administration of his estate and to advise her on several life insurance policies. Dave's estate was a simple one to complete as there were no children and everything was left to Jane. About a year after Dave's death, Jane sold their house and moved down to London.

'There's nothing to keep me here', she explained. 'I think it's best for me to make a completely new life for myself. I've got a job in the city and I'm leaving straight away. Thank you for everything you've done for me, Mr Francis.'

I heard no more from Jane after that, nor did I expect to do so. Many years later my secretary Clare - the one with the encyclopaedic memory for clients and cases - was telling me one dreary Monday morning of a visit she had made to some relations down south.

'We spent Saturday afternoon sightseeing in London, and who should I bump into in Piccadilly Circus but Jane Thomas. Do you remember her, Mr Francis? She was the young woman whose husband was killed in an accident on a building site? It's years ago now.'

'Yes, Clare', I replied, 'I remember her quite well.'

As I spoke I remembered the fortune-teller's prophecy and asked Clare almost instinctively:'

'How is she getting on?'

'She seems fine. She told me that she'd remarried some years ago and has two grown-up children.'

Coincidence some would no doubt say, pure coincidence. Maybe they are right, but as I remembered Jane telling me of the fortune-teller's prophecy, a very strange feeling came over me.

An even stranger feeling swept over me a few years later when I became involved in what started as a very run-of-the-mill case concerning a disputed right of way which ran through a small hamlet in a very remote part of the Dales. Now rural North Yorkshire has through the ages been an area known for superstition and for strange and eerie stories - a wilderness of moors and scours wild in the extreme, of lonely uplands and tumbled rocks, of old mine-shafts and quarries, miles of heather, of silences and echoes, and of underwater caverns and pot-holes feared longer than recorded time.

It was in the midst of such country that I set off one foggy and forbidding November day to see Fred Howes about the dispute which had flared up on his hill sheep farm.

A young London couple had bought a cottage which adjoined his farm for use at weekends and holidays, and had blocked off a path which ran through the small field in front of their cottage and which Fred had used for many years to get his sheep from one part of his farm to the other. There was nothing recorded in Fred's title deeds to prove the right of way, so I had to rely on what lawyers call 'prescription' to show that the right of way had been used without objection or interruption for upwards of thirty years. I took a statement from Fred and then went to see some of the locals, who all confirmed that the path had been used by Fred and those who farmed before him 'sin' Adam were a lad'. They nearly all remarked 'it were a shame owd Ned were no longer alive', because he had been the local authority on all footpaths, bridlepaths and rights of way in the area, and had spent much of his life walking them.

Back at my office, I decided that it would be useful for the court if there was a good set of photographs showing the right of way and where it actually ran. The professional photographer I engaged was a Denley friend of mine, George Browning, and he went off on his own to Fred's farm fully briefed as to what I actually required. A few days later, George appeared at my office with a large folder of the photographs under his arm. He looked rather puzzled as he handed them to me.

'It's very odd, Mr Francis', he said, "cos I'm sure there was no one actually using the path when I took the photos, but just look here.'

I looked at the first photo in George's folder, and saw at the end of the path what appeared to be the figure of a very old man dressed in a rather shabby overcoat and corduroys with a cloth cap and muffler, his bent frame supported by a stout walking stick.

'I don't remember that old man being there', commented George. 'In fact I'm sure he wasn't there. It's a quiet neck of the woods up there and it was absolutely deserted when I took the photos. Does it matter, Mr Francis - do you want me to take the photos again?'

'No, George, it doesn't matter.' I replied. 'In fact it's probably an advantage for the court to see a photo of the path with someone actually walking it.'

Later that day I showed the photographs to Fred, who had called in at my office to discuss the progress of his case.

'When dus tha reckon t' photo were tekken, Mr Francis?', he asked.

'George Browning took it earlier this week', I replied.

'Nay, Mr Francis, that can't be reight.'

'Why not?'

Fred looked at me rather strangely, and hesitated for a moment before whispering:

'Cos that's owd Ned in t' picture . . . an' it must be ovver five year sin 'e died, Ah reckon.'

Seeing 'owd Ned' in the photograph was a peculiar business indeed. But of all the strange experiences which have happened to me during my time as a country solicitor, undoubtedly the strangest of all occurred one dark January afternoon many years ago when I attended the offices of the old-established Dales firm of Arkwright and Sutton to complete a purchase.

Now in this day and age it is rare for a solicitor to have leave his office to complete a conveyancing transaction in person. The majority of legal titles are now registered at the Land Registry, so there is no longer any need to check through all the old deeds to make sure that the 'chain of ownership' is correct and complete before handing over a banker's draft for the purchase price.

It was all very different when I started in law. Back then I had to go to the offices of Arkwright and Sutton to 'do a completion' in the time-honoured way. I had in those days, as a newly qualified solicitor, not even heard of the firm of Arkwright and Sutton, whose office was situated just off the main street of the rather remote Dales market town of Grassdale. When I eventually arrived there, pulling up the collar of my raincoat to protect me from the chill east wind and icy rain which were sweeping down from the fells, I found myself facing an old stone-built property with steps up to the front door. At the side of it was a large brass plate with black lettering on it which read:

'Arkwright and Sutton

Solicitors and Commissioners for Oaths.'

Underneath was the inscription.

'J C Arkwright MA (Oxon).'

Whatever had happened to Mr Sutton? I wondered, as I went up the steps, rang the door bell and entered.

Truly, I thought as I closed the door behind me, I have entered the world of Charles Dickens and the lawyers he portrayed in his books. I was in a dingy, ill-lit reception area which even by the standards of those days was old-fashioned in the extreme. The floor was stone-flagged, there were bookcases crammed with dusty-looking leather-bound law reports, some faded *Spy* prints of old judges on the walls, and in the middle of the room was a curious piece of mahogany furniture which passed for a reception desk.

There did not seem to be a receptionist, and I was about to go outside and ring the bell again when a youngish man came in from the next room and asked if I would accompany him to his office. I found myself in another room which again might have come straight out of a Dickens novel. This time the stone-flagged floor was sloping, and much of the furniture, shelves and cabinets were tilting unevenly at various precarious-looking angles. There were more shelves of books and ancient law reports, and in the middle of the room was a rather splendid-looking partner's desk. The top of the desk was practically invisible, for it was covered by literally dozens of files, bundles of deeds and briefs to counsel tied with pink ribbon, and on top of these were various papers, letters and documents which did not appear to belong anywhere.

I wondered, as I gazed upon this disorderly and chaotic scene, how anything was ever found there. The clients of Arkwright and Sutton, I reflected, must have wondered too! My thoughts were interrupted by the young man who had accompanied me to the office. He introduced himself to me as Richard Clements and went on to say:

'I've just got to pop over to the bank for a few minutes. Do you mind if I leave you on your own till I get back? Here are the title deeds - perhaps you can be checking to see that they're all complete. I think you'll find they're all there.'

He then left the office. I started checking through the original deeds, comparing them against the summaries or what lawyers call 'abstracts of title' which were in my possession. There was hardly a sound in the building, except for the ticking of an old grandfather clock which stood in the passageway outside and the intermittent clacking of a typewriter somewhere upstairs. As I sat in the rather dingy light in front of the partner's desk, making somewhat slow progress with the job in hand, I could just see into the next room through a partly-opened doorway. In the middle of trying to decipher a barely legible handwritten deed of 1783, I heard a rustle of papers next door, looked up and saw an elderly man standing over a table, seemingly reading from a book. The light was bad, my view was partly obstructed, but what I saw quite clearly was an old man, nearly bald apart from a few strands of wispy grey hair. His body was long and thin, he was wearing a rather old-fashioned dark suit complete with waistcoat and gold Albert pocket watch, and he was peering at whatever he was reading through a pair of rather formidable-looking rimless glasses. He must, I reflected, have known that I was alone in the room next to him, but he made no move towards me. Out of politeness I was about to go through to introduce myself, when Richard Clements returned from his visit to the bank.

'Sorry to keep you, Mr Francis. Have you checked the deeds? Everything in order, I trust?'

'Yes, thank you, Mr Clements, the deeds are all present and correct. Here's a bank draft for the agreed price and I believe my clients are collecting the keys from the estate agent. I think that's everything.'

'It's been a pleasure, Mr Francis', replied my host.

'By the way', I said as I went back into the reception area and paused at the front door, 'who is the old gentleman I saw working at his desk in the office next to yours?'

'There's no one in that office, Mr Francis', replied the young solicitor, looking rather puzzled by my question. 'Can you describe him?'

I did so.

Richard Clements turned suddenly very pale.

'Mr Francis', he said, trembling slightly, 'the gentleman you have just described is old Mr Arkwright.'

'Your senior partner, I presume.'

'No, Mr Francis, I bought the practice from him six months ago. He was well past it in the last few years. As you can see he left everything in a frightful mess.'

At this point we both went quickly back into the room where I had seen Mr Arkwright working, but there was no one to be seen. The room was completely empty.

'Perhaps he'd just called back to collect something and went out the back way', I suggested as we walked back towards the office entrance.

'That's not possible', replied Mr Clements. 'You see, Mr Arkwright died three months ago.'

'Blood's Thicker Than Water'

It has often struck me forcibly over the years how often the most charming and delightful of men are married to ghastly women, and the loveliest and most intelligent girls choose the most scruffy and badly-behaved men as their partners.

Why old Colonel Eric Farnley had married such a plain, unattractive, snobbish and unpopular woman as Mildred Darnton was a complete mystery to the good Yorkshire people of Denley. According to his contemporaries, the Colonel - as he was universally known - had been quite a ladies' man: tall, good-looking, dashing and sporting, he was enormously attractive to the opposite sex. He could have picked a score of highly suitable brides, yet he chose the dreadful Mildred.

When I first knew the Colonel he had just retired. He had served in the Second World War with great courage and distinction and, like many of his friends who had enjoyed the male camaraderie of the army, he had not found it easy to adjust to civilian life. He was really much too honest to be a salesman, too naïve for business and unqualified for any of the professions.

An outdoors man if ever there was one, the Colonel found that he could not stand the confines of office life when an old friend invited him to join his insurance firm. He tried his hand at mushroom-growing, furniture-restoring and dog-breeding without much success, before finally ending up running a small nursery-cum-market garden on the outskirts of Denley. This was in the days long before garden centres became fashionable - and profitable. One thing was for sure: the Colonel never made much money.

When I first met him, the Colonel struck me as a most handsome and distinguished-looking man. Indeed, he even looked distinguished in his working clothes when I visited him at his market garden to advise on a contract for the delivery of some plants which had been called into question. He was always correctly dressed for the occasion. His suits were immaculate, his shirts carefully chosen to blend with his regimental tie, his shoes highly-polished, and his pure white hair matched the ever-present silk white handkerchief protruding from his breast pocket. His sartorial elegance was matched by a friendly, courteous manner. His courtesy went beyond simple politeness and good manners; it embraced a worldly tolerance of his fellow men and a genuine interest in their condition and welfare. He was especially noted for his chivalrous attitude towards the opposite sex. I see him now, raising his ever-present hat to any woman he met, be she duchess or char. In short, he was one of nature's gentlemen.

The Colonel had a friendly word for everyone. He was widely known in the Denley area, for he was involved in many local organisations - the parish church, St Johns Ambulance, life-saving, the British Legion - and was patron of just about every youth and sporting club in the district. In his younger days he had been a keen rugby player, but at the time I knew him all his spare time was devoted to the pursuit of the five great traditional rural pastimes enjoyed by country gentlemen from time immemorial: huntin', shootin', fishin', hawkin' and stalkin'.

The Colonel had always enjoyed riding to hounds, but in his latter years he was quite content to be field master of the local hunt, where his knowledge and love of the country, and tact with landowners made him an invaluable asset. If he was not out hunting, he was shooting pheasants or grouse - no party ever seemed complete without him. He was no stranger to the local trout rivers, but his chief delight was to join the 'chuck it and chance it' brigade in Scotland. A gleam would come into his eye as he talked of a forthcoming salmon trip. He also went north of the border stalkin' deer. That only left a limited amount of time for the fifth great country sport - hawkin' - but even this he managed now and again through the hospitality of an old army chum in the Middle East.

Two incidents illustrate the Colonel's character, the first of which I actually witnessed. It happened when, as a young solicitor, I attended an all-male sportsmen's dinner at a rather grand hotel a few miles out of Denley. I was sitting at the same table as the Colonel, and we were being attended by a very young waiter who looked barely old enough to have left school. He appeared so tense, nervous and ill-at-ease that I guessed he must have been doing his first job as a waiter. As, with shaky hands, he served the soup to each of us in turn, it was little short of a miracle that none of us needed to wipe clean our dinner suits. His luck did not last. The inevitable happened whilst our young waiter friend was serving the main course. Suddenly there was an almighty crash as dishes of peas and carrots slipped from his grasp, spilling the vegetables all over the table but with most of them ending up in the Colonel's lap.

Now many a man faced with such a disaster would, I suspect, have stood up, played merry hell and made a complaint to the manager, but not the Colonel. Without making any fuss whatsoever, he quietly wiped his dinner suit, smiled benignly at the by now petrified young waiter and simply said to him:

'It's jolly difficult, isn't it?'

The second incident from which the Colonel acquired almost folklore status in Denley was when he spectacularly rescued a middle-aged housewife from the clutches of a thuggish-looking youth who was after her handbag. The woman was desperately clinging on to her handbag, when the Colonel spotted her predicament from across the road and ran to her assistance. At this point he saw the youth had a flick knife, but the Colonel - trained in unarmed combat in the army - brought his walking stick down sharply on the robber's hand, forcing him to drop the knife on the pavement, before he knew what was happening. Instinctively the young thug bent down to pick it up, but before he could do so the Colonel's walking stick cracked down on his head. By this time a crowd was beginning to gather, and several men helped to detain the youth until the police arrived. As he was led handcuffed and ignominiously into a police van, people in the crowd who had watched this remarkable scene pushed forward to shake the Colonel's hand. Clearly embarrassed by the fuss, the Colonel simply pointed at the young thug in the back of the police van and quietly observed:

'Can't remember who said it, but it's true enough - "He who would be macho is generally not mucho".'

Now whilst the Colonel was held in universal respect, affection and esteem, his wife Mildred was arguably the most unpopular woman in Denley.

To start with, she possessed a voice which Yorkshire folk would in their politer moments describe as 'decided'. In truth it was harsh, loud and grating, and was made even worse by a rather 'put-on' posh accent. All in all, Mildred's voice was totally unbearable after a few minutes conversation. Then there were her clothes. It was no wonder the Colonel never had any money, for Mildred seemed to have a different outfit for every day and every occasion. But her best and most expensive of all she saved up for church which she attended diligently every Sunday. For her, this weekly ritual was not so much a religious experience as a fashion parade. Then again the Colonel's wife was a frightful name-dropper, always trying to ingratiate herself with those she considered to be the 'right sort of people'. How the Colonel used to wince when - anxious to impress the assembled company - she talked of a certain family.

'Very dear friends of ours', she would say affectedly, before pausing to add her favourite saying: 'Very wealthy people.'

Mildred was not only a frightful snob and a social climber of the worst kind, but she was a hypocrite too. She had a habit of walking through Denley after Sunday morning service and criticising people she spotted working in their gardens - tut-tutting as she went past and saying quite audibly: 'Gardening on the Lord's day of rest. Tut-tut - there'll be a reckoning you know.'

She was a hypocrite, for whilst criticising others for gardening on a Sunday, she herself employed a gardener who was very often seen digging Mildred's garden on that very day. She seemed totally oblivious to her double standards and continued in her high-handed ways.

When it came to going shopping, Mildred infuriated the locals by insisting on going to the front of the queue and demanding immediate service in her loud and unpleasant voice. It was no wonder the locals all referred to her as 'Lady Muck'.

Everyone who knew them was amazed that the Colonel was so tolerant of his wife's outrageous behaviour. She was a wittering woman if ever there was one, and she invariably bored any company she was in by her endless gossip, tittle-tattle and social pretensions. I suppose the Colonel just became accustomed to her over the years, dealing with their relationship by getting away from her as often as he could and when he was with her by simply switching off. One of his friends once asked him how on earth he had managed to stay with Mildred for so long. He shrugged his shoulders and replied simply: 'She's my wife, old boy.'

The Colonel paid a heavy price for his loyalty to Mildred. When they were in company, she deliberately set out to provoke him by demeaning him and telling everyone who would listen that it was a good job she had money of her own because he had never made any, and that he was no good for anything except the army. He was the archetypal hen-pecked husband, and there can have been little or no pleasure for him in his home life.

Mildred had her own solicitor, but the Colonel always came to consult me whenever he decided he needed a bit of legal advice on problems at his market garden. Not that he ever seemed particularly interested in discussing his legal position. In truth I suspect he looked upon a visit to my office as a good excuse to talk to me about his latest day's shooting or to try and tempt me to join him for a spot of fishing somewhere.

I had only just got to know the Colonel professionally when Mildred suddenly died of heart failure whilst still in her early fifties, an obese, unloved woman. I doubt whether anyone would have been at her funeral had it not been out of respect for the Colonel.

If the Colonel had problems with his wife, then they were as nought compared to those with his son Jeremy, who was as different in character to his father as it would be possible to imagine. Jeremy inherited his father's charm and good looks, but there the comparison ended. He cared nothing for his father's values and it was obvious from an early age that he would turn out badly.

The problems started at the expensive boarding school he attended, and from which he was expelled after having an affair with the local grocer's daughter and making her pregnant. She was the first in a long line of Jeremy's conquests. He eventually saved his parents further embarrassment by leaving Yorkshire and going to work in the City of London.

There, with the help of equally disreputable associates, he ran a succession of companies, all of which failed and all of which involved taking money from members of the general public which they never saw again. Jeremy's favourite ploy was to set up a company which was supposed to publish trade directories for various towns. He then proceeded to tout for subscriptions for advertisements in the directory, which he boasted would be widely circulated and available in all public places in the towns concerned. Needless to say, Jeremy never had the slightest intention of publishing a trade directory. He simply collected as much money as he could from prospective advertisers and then disappeared with it. Eventually the police caught up with him, and he served eighteen months in prison for obtaining money by false pretences. Prison was for him a university of crime, and he emerged from it more criminally sophisticated then ever.

Jeremy had always been spoilt rotten by his mother. Her decent and loyal husband she treated with disdain, but her thoroughly objectionable and dishonourable son she worshipped. In her eyes he could do no wrong. When he got into trouble, or as more frequently happened he got someone else into trouble, it was of course never her darling Jeremy's fault. At school she once told his open-mouthed teachers, whose tolerance of his insolence, bad manners and

141

discreditable behaviour had been strained beyond endurance, that they were all exceptionally honoured to have such a pupil at their school. When he was expelled from school for getting a girl pregnant, it was all the girl's fault of course for leading her Jeremy astray. It was the same when it came to her darling son's business ventures. It was as if she encouraged his big talk about offices, boardrooms, contracts and expensive cars. Of course it was always either bad luck or someone else's fault when every one of his businesses, built as they were on no more than big talk and castles of air, came crashing down, leaving a host of angry creditors and unpaid local tradespeople. Even when Jeremy went to prison and broke his father's heart, she proclaimed the injustice of it. Of course her darling son was going to publish the trade directory - he just wasn't given enough time.

Soon after Jeremy came out of prison, his mother died. Jeremy had sponged on his parents mercilessly for years, so by the time his mother died, all her money had gone on bailing him out of his many and varied financial difficulties. The Colonel's money had nearly all gone too. All he was left with was his small house, his modest army pension, and his run-down nursery business which was on rented land and worth very little.

Jeremy was typical of many only chidren - spoilt, always coming first in everything and used to getting his own way. Not content with having squandered all his mother's money, Jeremy carried on sponging from his father after her death. 'Blood's thicker than water, old boy', the Colonel would say as he tried to explain to concerned friends his continuing generosity to his wayward son. He must surely have known that there was little or no chance of any of the loans to his son being repaid.

The final blow fell after the Colonel had been persuaded by his son to guarantee a bank loan to finance the launch of yet another ill-starred business venture. So tired by this time was he of all his son's finacial shenanigans, the Colonel neither took proper independent legal advice nor even bothered to read the document before he signed. Disastrously, as it turned out, the guarantee he gave was a legal mortgage over his house and was to cover all borrowings made by his son. Within eighteen months the business had failed. On the day when the bank finally pulled the plug, Jeremy was overdrawn to the tune of £150,000 and he had absolutely no means of repaying such a sum. The bank called in his father's guarantee. It was only then that the Colonel finally came to see me and asked for advice on his legal position. There was nothing I could do for him.

'A guarantee is guarantee, I'm afraid, Colonel. I wish you'd come to see me earlier. You know I'd have advised you against giving any sort of financial assistance to your son based on his past record, but if you'd insisted I'd have done my damndest to persuade you not to give the bank your house as security. I always say to people: give them insurance policies, shares, anything, so long as you don't give them your home.'

'Too late now, Francis', replied the Colonel, who invariably adopted the public school and army tradition of calling other men by their surname. 'Don't know what I'll do now. Rather a pickle old boy, wouldn't you say?'

I simply nodded in agreement. The Colonel had lost everything - his wife, his money and his house. There was nothing I could see in his future but a bleak and poverty-stricken old age.

I was surprised, therefore, to hear only a short time afterwards that the Colonel was living happily on the outskirts of Denley in a little cottage which suited all his needs down to the ground. A country solicitor hears most of the local gossip and tittle-tattle one way or another, and it was not long before my curiosity as to how the Colonel had come by the cottage was satisified. It turned out that the good lady who had been saved from robbery and assault by the Colonel's decisive use of his walking stick all those years ago had heard of his plight at exactly the same time she had inherited a small cottage, for which she had no particular use. She went to see him.

'One good turn deserves another, Colonel', she said when he protested at her generosity. 'You can live there as long as you like and I don't want any rent. I owe my life to you.'

When I heard what had happened, on what had been a particularly difficult day at the office dealing with awkward and disagreeable people, I felt that my faith in human nature had been restored. The Colonel happily lived out the rest of his life in the cottage . . . and someone told me recently that Jeremy was last sighted hop-picking in Kent.

A Village Tale For Our Times

The Dales villages I have known and loved all my life are changing, in some cases out of all recognition. Unsightly developments and the tawdry aspects of tourism have played their part, but perhaps the biggest change to the character and atmosphere of the villages has been brought about by the growing influx of commuters and weekenders - people without roots in rural life, and with no feel for country ways and traditions.

At one time, in Dales villages, everyone knew everyone else, but nowadays when I visit people in these places they frequently complain to me that they don't know half the people living there.

What is worse, many of the 'off comed-uns' alienate the locals by bringing with them suburban attitudes and try to impose a way of life from which they, the newcomers, dreaming of a country idyll, have apparently tried to escape! For a start they try to tidy everyone up - and if there's one thing true country people can't stand, it's being tidied up.

My old friend Billy Nixon, a retired jobbing builder in the Dales village of Linburn, was surprised and delighted at the price he was offered for his stone-built cottage on the main street. James and Audrey Newcome (a surname the villagers thought highly appropriate) had lived in the suburbs of Leeds all their lives, but had long shared a dream of owning 'a cottage in the country'. When they saw Billy's cottage advertised they rushed out to see it, immediately fell in love with it and made Billy the best offer he had ever had in his life. James and Audrey saw their ideal of rural bliss at last coming true - a dream cottage with roses round the door, a picture-postcard village which stays the same forever, a place where people live in harmony with nature, an idyllic community where everyone loves and cares for one another.

As Billy told me all about the purchasers of his old cottage, I thought that they would very soon discover that the reality of rural life is and always has been very different to the dream.

The transaction was completed in the summer, but it was not until late autumn when James and Audrey moved in to their newly-acquired property. By this time the appearance of the house and the garden had been completely transformed.

Now Billy's cottage was, it has to be admitted, a bit run-down and, from the point of view of a suburbanite, his garden was rather untidy. There were lots of roses and mossy paths concealed by all sorts of old-fashioned flowers, but pride of place was given to a potato patch; Billy loved to work in it, as villagers stopped on their way down the street, leant over the fence and discussed important matters with him like maincrop, back-earlies and blight.

James and Audrey left the roses round the door, but changed nearly everything else. They put in bow windows, new doors with chiming bells and mock carriage-lanterns. In the garden the first thing they did was to pull down the fence adjoining the village street. They then replaced Billy's simple garden of flowers and potatoes with a large lawn newly laid out, at great expense, with the best Cumberland sea-washed turf. Around it was a border filled with geraniums and other formal bedding-out plants. The result was a typical suburban garden, one designed for appearance rather than for pleasure and the kitchen.

Perhaps this was not altogether surprising, as both James and Audrey had lived all their lives in the suburbs. James had been a civil servant and his spare time had been devoted mainly to his local golf club, where he played with the same cronies two or three times a week. Audrey had never been in paid employment, but had devoted her time outside the family to various charities and local causes. She was a committee woman *par excellence*. A basically decent and well-meaning person, she was nevertheless a do-gooder of the worst kind, one who liked having a finger in every pie and always interfering in matters which would have been better left alone.

The first thing which took James and Audrey by surprise when they arrived in the village was that Linburn proved to be noisier than the Leeds suburb from which they had come. They had not taken up residence for more than a week before Audrey had complained to the vicar about the sound of the church bells disturbing her Sunday morning lie-in. The vicar's reaction was rather more diplomatic that that of neighbouring farmer Fred Rodley when the couple complained about the noise of his cows mooing and cockerels crowing. The strong Anglo-Saxon words uttered by Fred were also surely in the mind of Jim Bryson, proprietor of the old-established village riding stables, when Audrey complained to him about horse droppings in the road outside her cottage. He managed not to utter them, but his reply worried the Newcomes even more:

'You should see the road after t' hunt's held its annual Boxing Day meet.'

News of James and Audrey's complaints to the vicar and to Fred and Jim quickly spread through the village. Many tongues were soon wagging, and knowing nods, winks and smiles were exchanged. They did not have to wait long for the next incident to set them talking. It concerned the couple's septic tank.

James and Audrey had never owned a septic tank before and knew nothing whatever about them. They had been assured when they bought the cottage that it was in good working order, and they had thought no more about it.

On moving into the cottage, they had devoted much time and energy in cleaning and decorating the property to an impeccable standard, but in doing so they had flushed large quantities of bleach and detergent down the lavatory. Now Billy Nixon was a countryman who knew how septic tanks worked, and he took care that the only thing he flushed down the lavatory occasionally was a little yeast. The septic tank, which had lain quiescent and caused no problems for old Billy in thirty-odd years, reacted violently to the bacteria-destroying liquids flushed into it by James and Audrey. Soon a horrible smell pervaded the whole village. The Newcomes had no idea why this had happened and couldn't understand why the locals seemed to find it so amusing. They didn't seem too helpful about the problem either.

'Tricky things is septic tanks', was about the best they could get out of any of them.

The smell from the septic tank was the first problem the Newcomes were to endure, but it was very quickly followed by another more serious one.

Now anyone who has ever lived in the country knows the value of walls and fences. For one thing, they form a barrier against straying sheep and cattle.

James and Audrey's neighbouring Fred Rodley, with whom they had already exchanged words over the noise made by his farm animals, had not realised when he drove his herd down the village street to pastures new that the fence adjoining the Newcomes' garden had been taken down. Before he could do anything about it, his cows were trampling all over James and Audrey's expensively manicured lawn and flower borders. This disaster occurred, as ill-luck would have it, after two days of continuous rain. By the time Fred had regained control of his herd, his cows had turned the whole front garden into a muddy, dung-littered morass.

This sad event was quickly the talk of the village and, truth to tell, it attracted little sympathy from the locals. Fred Rodley, who had already been rubbed up the wrong way by the Newcome's earlier complaints, was quite forthright in his opinion:

'An oppen-plan garden? An oppen-plan garden?', he repeated. 'Whoever 'eard of an oppen-plan garden in t' country? That were an accident waitin' tae 'appen, Ah reckons.'

After their problem with the septic tank and Fred's cows, the Newcomes' dream of a rural idyll was beginning to turn into a nightmare, but they were not yet willing to throw in the towel. After talking things over, they decided to try and live out their dream by throwing themselves wholeheartedly into village life, which they fondly imagined would be a community of 'caring and sharing'. They were soon, however, to learn a rapid and painful lesson about the reality of village politics.

Little did James and Audrey realise when, in the absence of any other volunteers, they became members of the village hall committee, that they were to find themselves right in the middle of two distinct factions which had bitterly opposed each other for years.

The first, led by octogenarian village elder Sam Poppleton, was against any proposal which would involve change of any kind whatsoever. Sam's standard and classic reply to any such proposal invariably started with the words:

'In this village we've always . . . '

The second faction was led by ambitious local builder and parish councillor Ronnie Hazel. He had always resented Sam's power in village affairs and he thought that Sam had contrived to thwart several potentially lucrative development proposals; so Ronnie automatically opposed any position taken by Sam and his friends. The Newcomes saw what they thought was a golden opportunity to pour oil on troubled waters - only to find that their well-meant interventions during committee meetings merely served to unite the two factions against them.

'You two haven't bin 'ere five minutes and 'ere you are tellin' us 'ow tae go on', thundered Ronnie.

James and Audrey reeled back in their chairs, astonished by this attack, before turning to face the inevitable lecture from Sam:

'In this village we've always . . . '

James and Audrey found no consolation at the Linburn Arms when they called in for a drink after the meeting. If they were looking for a stimulating intellectual discussion with like-minded people of progressive views, they were to be sadly disappointed. The talk among the locals seemed to revolve around sheep and cattle, hunting, shooting and fishing, and who was carrying on with whom. They didn't go in the pub again after that.

As their first winter wore on, James and Audrey found themselves becoming even more unpopular in the village. This wasn't helped when they led the opposition to a proposal for a small business development on a site at the end of the village. Their opposition was only supported by other 'off comed-uns' like themselves and weekenders who wanted the village to be kept exactly as it was. The locals, however, took an entirely different view. They knew that, with the drift from the land and the recent closure of the only working quarry in the dale, there was little work for young men and the proposed development meant a real opportunity for them.

They then tried - without success - to redeem themselves in the eyes of the villagers by joining in moves to save the village shop when the owners talked about closing it; but as one or two locals were quick to observe, James and Audrey rarely shopped in the village but went into town each week to buy their groceries at the supermarket.

By the time the Newcomes had got through their first winter at Linburn, they found themselves deeply unpopular in the village, and also far from happy in their cottage. In particular James, who was a tall man, kept banging his head on the beams which he had at first sight found so attractive, and was discovering that the cottage was much smaller and darker than he had imagined. One day, in a fit of pique after banging his head on a beam in the lounge yet again, he decided to have the floor lowered. This was an expensive and disruptive business, and hardly had the work been completed than there was a week of heavy rain. At the end of the week, James and Audrey were in bed, when Audrey suddenly said:

'Can you hear something? It sounds like water downstairs.'

When they went down to investigate, they found their lounge under a foot of water, carpet and curtains ruined, and antique furniture and ornaments badly stained. It took them a month to clean up and sort out the insurance. James found that there was a well under the floor which had overflowed, and he had to install an expensive pump system to avoid a repetition of the disaster.

By this time the Newcomes were nearly at the end of their tether. But it was summer again, the dale was looking at its pastoral best, and they decided to carry on. They were just beginning to think that their troubles were over when another disaster befell them, a disaster which was to prove the last straw.

James and Audrey repositioned the fireplace when they had their lounge floor lowered, but they had never burnt a real coal or wood fire - Audrey thinking it too dirty - and so installed an artificial one instead. They had forgotten to block up the chimney, although they had taken the precaution of stuffing newspaper up it to guard against a fall of soot.

One summer evening as they were sitting in their lounge, Audrey was sure she heard a rustle from somewhere up the chimney.

'Did you hear anything just then?', she asked her husband.

'No', replied James. 'I can't hear anything. It must be your imagination.'

'Just be quiet and listen again', said Audrey.

This time there was another louder rustle which neither of them could mistake.

'There's definitely something up the chimney', repeated Audrey. 'It must be a bird that's got stuck.'

'I suppose you want me to deal with it', said James reluctantly.

James took off his jacket, pulled up his shirt sleeve, and rather gingerly started to put his hand up the chimney and pull out the pieces of newspaper which were wedged up there.

As he pulled away the last piece of newspaper, there was a sudden shower of soot which made him jump back in surprise and alarm. This was followed by another bigger shower of soot, which fell on the hearth and then flew in all directions, covering at least half of the lounge carpet which had so recently been cleaned after the overflow from the well. As James and Audrey stood back looking in horror at the scene before them, and at the sooty mess on the carpet, they both suddenly spotted the cause of the disaster.

There in the middle of the hearth stood a little owl, covered in soot from head to foot, and blinking in the sudden light.

'Isn't he sweet', said Audrey, forgetting for a minute the shocking state of the room caused by the huge soot fall.

She leaned forward to stroke the bird's head, but before she could even touch it, the owl turned and pecked her savagely on her wrist, drawing blood.

At this point Audrey ran from the cottage, sobbing hysterically. James followed her out and neither would return until old Ned Forshaw, a retired farm worker who lived a few doors away, had gone into the cottage and had removed the little owl and released it into a nearby wood.

I heard a blow-by-blow account of the Newcomes' mishap with the little owl from Ned Forshaw himself, and he went on to tell me about their other misfortunes since they had bought their 'dream' cottage from old Billy Nixon.

'Aye', said Ned, 'it's like Ah've allus said: "Off comed-uns" 'ave tae be wintered, summered and wintered agin afore we can reckon up if they'll be stayin'. Ah'll be fair capp'd missen if them that 'as owd Billy's place stop 'ere much longer.'

Ned's words proved to be prophetic.

The last I heard of James and Audrey was that they had put their cottage on the market and were contemplating moving to a flat in Ilkley or Harrogate - somewhere close to the town centre, handy for the shops, near to a golf course and not far from Audrey's mother!

Epilogue
A Cold Wind Blowing

On the day I finished writing the last story in this book, I took a stroll down Denley High Street. I couldn't help but reflect not only on the physical changes which had taken place in the town and its surrounding villages since my boyhood, but also on the disappearance of so many of the characters associated with them who have featured in my stories. It seemed to me, as I pulled up my coat collar, that all too many of the familiar and ancient landmarks had gone, gone with the icy cold wind which was blowing in my face.

Above all I noticed once again that most of the friendly, small shopkeepers had disappeared. When I was a boy, every Yorkshire town and city was distinguished by its own highly individual clutch of family-run shops and businesses.

Leeds, for instance, I chiefly remember for its splendid department stores such as Lewis's, Schofields and Matthias Robinsons, for the period charm of J Dyson and Sons, jewellers, where I bought my wife's engagement ring, Herbert Sutcliffe's, where I bought my first cricket bat, and for the character of the old market. In Bradford it was Brown and Muffs, and Woods, the record and musical instrument shop. On those very special Saturday mornings when my mother took me to the exclusive and elegant town of Harrogate, she would be immaculately dressed for the occasion, complete with hat and gloves.

We would visit such splendid shops as Hudsons, Wrays, Hitchens, Allens, the gentlemen's outfitters *par excellence*, and always Standings, where I bought Harrogate toffee with hard-saved pocket money and where my godmother once treated me to morning coffee and afterwards smilingly slipped into my hand one of those wonderfully large white five pound notes. I felt like a millionaire.

In my own home town of Denley there was James the tobacconist, who proudly displayed what must surely have been the finest and most varied selection of pipe-tobacco mixture to be found anywhere in Yorkshire. His shop happily still survives, but Fossets, the splendid family grocers which I shall forever associate with the smell of freshly-ground coffee, has long since gone, along with Mrs Harbottle's 'olde sweet shoppe', Ivor Westgate's where I bought my first school satchel, the pet shop where my wife as a young girl sold her baby budgies, and Franklin Elder's bookshop with its wonderful collection of cricket literature.

154

As I walked down the High Street with my memories, it was uncomfortable to have to accept that all these familiar shops had gone forever, along with the town's two cinemas and the best residential hotel where property auctions had for years been held in civilised and agreeable surroundings.

The reason for my walk along the High Street was to call in at the closing-down sale of Fortescue and Son - the last gentlemen's outfitters in the town. When I was a boy there were lots of shops like Fortescues. They were to be found in just about every town of any size and they all looked very much the same. There were always glass tops on the counters with trays of beautiful silk ties, and there were handkerchiefs and gloves in sliding shelves underneath. Behind the counter were heavy, dark mahogany cabinets where row after row of suits, tweeds and sports jackets hung from brass rails. Nearby there was sometimes a hand-crafted Victorian wooden horse for children to ride on, and on the wall somewhere there was more often then not a photograph of some local agricultural show in which gentlemen wearing traditional country clothes were to be seen inspecting prizewinning sheep and cattle. Presiding over such shops was a unique breed of proprietor - generally a husband and wife team - who were respectful to the point of being deferential and who were unfailingly polite, cheerful, courteous and helpful.

These shops always carried an incredible amount of stock; customers were not only spoilt for choice but could invariably find something which was highly individual. I remember once discovering to my intense delight a splendid old-fashioned police mackintosh whilst rummaging in a store room. Even the polite proprietor could not resist smiling when I tried it on, but it was I who smiled in the years to come when it kept me dry in many a winter storm.

As I took a last lingering look at Fortescue's shop, and bought a traditional tweed jacket at a knock-down price for old time's sake, I could not help but feel nostalgic at the prospect of such a splendid shop disappearing from Denley for ever, and sentimental at the thought of the passing of a way of business based not purely on the profit motive but on trust, honest dealing and friendship.

As I walked on down the street from Fortescues, I noticed yet again that where once the High Street had been dominated by lots of highly individual family-owned shops and businesses, now only a few remained, sandwiched beween empty premises disfigured by 'For Sale' signs, building society and estate agents' offices, chain stores and charity shops. Most of the old shops have been victims of the modern age, crippled by ridiculously high rents and rates, patronised by folk who are too busy for a smile and a chat, and who no longer value a polite personal service, and finally being unable to compete with the large soulless supermarkets which have mushroomed everywhere.

Truly there is a cold wind blowing. It is one which is not just affecting the small shopkeepers but many of their traditional customers too, particularly in the farming community. Some of the cattle markets in the Dales, which have been the scene of regular auctions for hundreds of years as well as being a meeting place for country people, have already closed and others are in financial difficulties. This is of no surprise when one considers the present-day problems of the hill sheep men and small farmers in the surrounding dales, who are having all on just to survive and continue their way of life.

The day after my depressing stroll along Denley High Street, the problems of the local community were forcibly brought to my attention when I visited two farmers up the dale.

I had called to see old Charlie Fixby to talk to him about milk quotas and 'set aside'. Charlie had seen many changes over the years, but being restricted by the Government as to his milk production when he had previously been encouraged to expand his herd seemed utterly illogical; and as for 'set aside', it was just plain daft, to his way of thinking, that farmers should actually be paid for growing docks and thistles.

I always enjoy chatting to Charlie about the old days in farming. When Charlie's father was still alive he liked to join in the discussions, giving anyone who was prepared to listen the benefit of his views about farming during the last war. Charlie's father didn't like change very much, and he particularly liked holding forth on the subject of artificial insemination, which he contended was contrary to nature and no substitute for breeding his own stock from his own bull. He enjoyed quoting a rather rude rhyme about it, composed during the war by some farmer with a sense of humour, in which a cow complained sadly:

'These Land Army tarts
That play with my parts
Still have it the old-fashioned way.'

After Charlie had reminisced a bit about his father, we laughed together as he related some of the amusing incidents of days long past. Then he suddenly became serious and shook his head sadly.

'T' job's gitten to t' stage wheer it's not worth carryin' on, Ah reckons. Payin' farmers tae do nowt wi t' land.' Charlie shook his head again. 'There's nobbut t' missus an' me now, an' Ah reckons we're about ready tae pack t' job in.'

I got much the same reaction when I went a bit further up the dale and walked with my long-standing friend Jimmy Lindley around his hill sheep farm.

'Ignorance an' prejudice, Mr Francis, that's what we've tae contend wi these days - tek a look at this.'

I looked at the newspaper Jimmy was asking me to read, and skimmed quickly through a letter to the editor from a lady vegetarian who was advocating that Dales farmers should keep sheep for their fleeces rather than their meat.

'Aye, Mr Francis, its a bad enuf job as it is tryin' tae mek owt. Ah'd jus like tae see t' lady mekkin' a livin' out o' t' fleeces. Ah reckons she 'asn't a bloody clue as to what soart o' brass she'd be gittin' frae fleeces. There's a cold wind blowin', tha knows. It's t' worst Ah can remember in t' sheep job, an' if yon woman thinks t' salvation is in bloody fleeces . . . '

Jimmy paused for a minute to catch his breath as his face grew redder and he stabbed the newspaper with his fingers.

'It jus goes tae show that she 'asn't t' fust idea as tae price t' fleeces are fetchin'. Dus yon woman want tae see all t' farmers eatin' grass along wi' t' sheep?' Jimmy shook his head in disbelief and paused for a minute before carrying on. 'These people as cum to t' dales , Mr

Francis, like lookin' at sheep in t' fields like it were theer god-given right, but if women like that 'ave theer way, there bloody soon won't be any more sheep in t' dales, Ah reckons. An' t' way t' job is now, t' next generation won't be sheep-farmin' anyroad. Ah doubts they'll put up wi t' soart o' life me father an' me 'as 'ad: nowt but work, more work an' no brass at t' finish, out in all weathers, seven days a week - an' for what? Them townies 'at write letters to t' papers 'aven't t' fust idea about t' job, Ah reckons. Aye, like Ah said, Mr Francis, it's a cold wind blowin'.'

I was still thinking about the future of the small shopkeepers, the hill sheep farmers and my other clients and friends facing similar economic hard times, as I made my way down the dale and back to the office.

I looked at the brass plate fixed to the wall at the side of the entrance and could not help but reflect, too, on the future of the traditional family solicitor. I was struck again by the depressing thought that his future appears not so very different from that of his clients. Like it or not, the great profession which my generation of solicitors entered with a sense of enthusiasm and pride is no more. We have all been pitched headlong into the market place. Bankers, building societies and financial institutions are entering our traditional areas of work, like tax planning, probate, wills and even conveyancing. At the same time, drastic reductions in the legal aid scheme are being implemented and the expenses of running a practice rise inexorably from year to year.

When I first became a partner, not as much attention needed to be paid to the financial side of running an office. At that time we solicitors were assured of making a reasonable living. The understanding was that by hard work, study and passing difficult examinations we had become members of a learned profession, a privilege which provided us with the opportunity to serve and help the people of our own communities. Nowadays, I reflected, solicitors like myself could only continue to survive by dint of rigorous daily attention to financial management and control. Add to these truths the fact that the majority of young solicitors are drifting increasingly to the large commercial firms in the city, and the traditional family or country solicitor looks an increasingly endangered species. How soon, I wondered, would we too disappear, along with the small shopkeepers, the hill sheep farmers, the huntin', shootin', fishin' types, the characters of rural life like 'Capstan' Carter and Franklin Elders, and the host of other country folk who have supported our special kind of legal practice?

Not for much longer, I fear, will there be the 'local solicitor' rooted in and committed to the local community, a friend in times of trouble, a person with a wide experience of life and law to give sound advice based on a personal knowledge of the family in question, a family solicitor, not just a purveyor of legal services.

The week after I had finished writing this book had been thoroughly depressing. I could not remember a time during my practising career when so many of my clients were in difficulties: financial worries, business closures, tenants not paying their rents, new ventures failing, bankruptcies, redundancy and unemployment, all of these disasters ironically leading to the only two growth areas in our practice - crime and divorce. A cold wind blowing indeed!

It was a Friday and I was the last to leave the office. Even the prospect of the weekend ahead did nothing to lift my feeling of depression and anxiety for the future. I had one more call to fit in on the way home before calling it a day.

Jake Morris and his wife Nora were both semi-invalids and well into their eighties. Life had not been easy for either of them. They had suffered the tragedy of losing their only son in a car crash. Jake had been made redundant by the small mill where he had always worked, and at a time when he could no longer find another job. As a consequence they were both very poor and their declining years had been clouded further by illness. They helped each other as best they could, but without the support of their home help and their kindly neighbours they would most certainly have had to go into an old folk's home.

As I let myself in through the door they were both sitting huddled by a small fire and watching the news on television. As so often seems to be the case these days, it was full of wars, death, tragedy and starvation all over the world, an unremitting diet of gloom and doom.

'It's being so cheerful as keeps 'em going', said Jake, and all three of us laughed.

The news on television had been as gloomy as the last few days at the office had been, but as I made my way home, the courage and cheerfulness of Jake and Nora were already perceptibly lightening my depression. I felt somehow that my mood was about to change.

It is funny how at difficult times the old familiar expressions of childhood return. 'These things are sent to try us', my Scottish granny used to say, and 'You'll see things differently in the morning'.

It is true. I woke up the next day feeling refreshed. Overnight the driving rain had cleared to the east and the cold wind which had been blowing all week had suddenly dropped. The weather can change as quickly in the Dales as the feelings of the human heart.

All my life I have found that the best antidote to depression is a good long walk in the Dales. Richard Jefferies, perhaps the greatest and surely the most spiritual of all English writers in the rural tradition, knew the value of the countryside to the human psyche:

'No matter how kind their parents may be, no matter how fortunate their circumstances, the children in cities never know the joyousness of the country'.

In his wonderfully evocative book *The Dewy Morn*, Jefferies went on to address his reader in these memorable words, arguably the noblest and truest he ever wrote.

'All of you with little children and who have no need to count expense or even if you have such need, take them somehow to the country, among green grass and yellow wheat, among trees and by hills and streams if you wish their highest education, that of the heart and soul, to be completed'.

As I set off on my walk I marvelled again at the timeless beauty of the Dales, even on a Saturday in late November. How right Jefferies was, I reflected. People are so preoccupied with money and business and property. We worship at the altar of Mammon too much these days.

160

I pondered, too, on the fact that there have been equally hard times or even harder times for past generations of Dalesfolk. Life for our rural forebears was undoubtedly poorer, tougher and shorter than our own. I thought again about my small farmer clients as I surveyed the rural landscape made beautiful purely as a result of their labour and love of the land. The 1930s had been a desperate time for them, a time when landlords had to reduce rents to enable their tenants to survive and to keep the land in production. Please God we do not have to suffer another war before things improve.

As I stopped for a few minutes, lit my pipe, reflected upon the essential truth of Jefferies' writing and surveyed once more the timeless beauty of my particular part of the Yorkshire Dales, my thoughts were disturbed by the familiar voice of Nathaniel Jackson, a retired farmer. Nat, I knew, was approaching his ninetieth birthday but, although a little bent and frail now, was still strong enough to take a three mile walk every day.

'Na then, lad', he said, using the well-known Yorkshire expression as a form of greeting.

'Good morning, Mr Jackson. I've just stopped to admire the view.'

As we fell into conversation, I realised with some humility that I was talking to a man who had lived through two world wars, had seen economic hard times before, and all the ups and downs of farming in the Dales.

'Aye, lad', he concluded, 'it's a struggle on t' farms but it's nowt to what it were once ovver. Ah've seen it afore tha knows. 'Appen soon it'll be right. Aye, lad, it'll be right.'

My walk in the countryside and my talk with Nat had, by the time I got home, enabled me to see economic hard times in a better historical perspective and to take a more optimistic view. As I sat by my fireside that evening I poured myself a glass of wine, put on a treasured record of Josef Locke singing *Count your Blessings One by One* and cheerfully concluded that, although times might be tough and an era might be ending for country solicitors and their clients, not even the coldest of cold economic winds could chill the warmth of the human spirit. The Dales way of life would after all endure at least

for as long as there was friendship and fellowship, love, labour and laughter, and an old farmer still there to greet me and say:
'It'll be reight, lad. Aye it'll be reight.'

18/12